BUILDING COMMITMENT

A Leader's Guide to Unleashing
the Human Potential at Work

SECOND EDITION

CARL WELTE

Copyright © 2022 Carl Welte.

All rights reserved. No part of this book may be reproduced, stored, or transmitted by any means—whether auditory, graphic, mechanical, or electronic—without written permission of both publisher and author, except in the case of brief excerpts used in critical articles and reviews. Unauthorized reproduction of any part of this work is illegal and is punishable by law.

ISBN: 979-8-88640-253-7 (sc)
ISBN: 979-8-88640-254-4 (hc)
ISBN: 979-8-88640-255-1 (e)

Because of the dynamic nature of the Internet, any web addresses or links contained in this book may have changed since publication and may no longer be valid. The views expressed in this work are solely those of the author and do not necessarily reflect the views of the publisher, and the publisher hereby disclaims any responsibility for them.

One Galleria Blvd., Suite 1900, Metairie, LA 70001
1-888-421-2397

Also by Carl Welte

*Making and Fulfilling Your Dreams as a Leader:
A Practical Guide for Formulating and Executing Strategy*

*Communicating about Differences:
Understanding, Appreciating, and Talking
about Divergent Points of View*

To our six wonderful grandchildren, Jake, Ben Kayla, Zach, Ashley, and Calvin, and our great granddaughter, Charlotte, who provide my wife Dee and I tremendous joy and pride. It is marvelous to be witness to their learning and growth+. They will each discover their own purposes and destinies and make important contributions.

CONTENTS

Preface to the Second Edition ix
Acknowledgments xi
Introduction xiii

1. Building Commitment:
   The Business Case for Doing So 1
2. Understanding Motivation:
   Commitment versus Compliance 7
3. Building Block #1:
   Selection: Choosing the Right People 22
4. Building Block #2:
   Clarity: Developing Shared Expectations 60
5. Building Block #3:
   Performance Coaching: Guiding Success 112
6. Building Block #4:
   Teams: Synergy at Work 162

Conclusion 225
Appendix A: The Alex Reed Case 228
Appendix B: Team Assessment 239
Endnotes 249
About the Author 255

PREFACE TO THE SECOND EDITION

This new and improved edition of *Building Commitment* incorporates the increased wisdom and knowledge I have gained regarding building cultures of commitment since the initial version was published in 2016.

Enhancements have been made throughout the book to provide greater clarity relative to understanding and applying the components of building and sustaining a culture of commitment as contrasted with a culture of compliance.

ACKNOWLEDGMENTS

I am grateful to the many organizations for which I have worked as a leader or consultant and the challenging opportunities they have afforded me to learn and grow and acquire my knowledge of leadership and organizational effectiveness. I am also grateful to the wonderful people who have provided me valuable learning experiences, mentoring, and coaching along the way.

One of the things I have always cherished about leadership and organizational consulting and coaching is that each engagement is unique allowing for growth adding greater value to my clients.

INTRODUCTION

> Perhaps the most promising trend in our thinking about leadership is the conviction that the purposes of the group are best served when the leader helps followers to develop their own initiative, strengthen the use of their own judgment, and enable them to grow and to become better contributors.
>
> —John W. Gardiner

There are two imperatives for assuring sustained organization success.

The first imperative is a *sound strategy*. A strategy that clearly articulates both the organization's *Identity*, "Who we are"; and, "What we stand for"; and *Direction*, "Where we are going"; "What it looks like when we get there"; and, "How we are going to get there."

The second imperative is a work culture that fosters *genuine commitment*. A committed workforce is one where people "want to perform" rather than feeling that they "have to perform", which is compliance. A committed workforce is one in which people want to work together to struggle to achieve shared aspirations. That is right, struggle. A committed workforce realizes that anything worth striving for does not come easy. They are motivated to do whatever it takes to work toward achieving important shared aspirations.

My book *Making and Fulfilling Your Dreams as a Leader: A Practical Guide for Formulating and Executing* Strategy[1] addresses the first imperative. Its purpose is to enable you as a leader, regardless of organizational level or business sector, to formulate and execute a sound strategy. The book equips you with a strategic framework to use on an ongoing basis to establish and live your organizational identity and direction in the face of current and emerging realities.

This book, *Building Commitment; A Leader's Guide to Unleashing the Human Potential at Work*, addresses the second imperative, building and maintaining a work culture that fosters commitment. It is a natural follow on to *Making and Fulfilling Your Dreams as a Leader*.

A committed or engaged workforce is a productive workforce, which is critical for achieving desired business results. This should not come as a shock to you or anyone. And increasingly there is solid research results backing up this axiom.

But despite the pivotal role an engaged workforce plays in achieving desired business results, ongoing research results tell us that there is a significant gap in most organizations between potential and actual human performance. This gap is caused by organizations and their leaders not doing what it takes to develop a sound strategy and fostering a work culture of commitment to effectively execute that strategy.

The purpose of this book is to equip you the leader, again, regardless of business sector or organizational level, with the clarity, confidence, and competence to foster a work culture of commitment. Doing so is, of course, easier if you are fortunate to be a part of an organization that understands the importance of and works at building a

INTRODUCTION

motivating environment. But regardless of the larger context, your role as a local leader is paramount in building commitment. For it is you, their leader, who your people rely on to establish a sound strategy, translate what is going on for them, and help them succeed in doing their part in contributing to the greater good.

This book provides you with a logical and comprehensive path for building a work culture that fosters commitment. In addition, the individual chapters stand on their own, serving as a continuing and valuable resource for you.

The first two chapters, *Building Commitment: The Business Case for Doing So* and *Understanding Motivation: Commitment versus Compliance* provide an important context for what follows.

The remaining four chapters present the specific building blocks in logical order for building commitment. It all starts with selecting the right people, the subject of chapter 3. Next comes clarity, brought about by developing shared expectations, the focus of chapter 4. Chapter 5 covers the importance of guiding success through ongoing performance coaching. And finally in chapter 6, realizing the synergy that can be realized by creating high-performing teams.

Practical and proven concepts, structures, practices, processes, and tools, as well as exercises, are provided throughout the book to help you immediately apply what you are learning.

1. BUILDING COMMITMENT: THE BUSINESS CASE FOR DOING SO

> Getting extraordinary things done in organizations is hard work. The climb to the summit is arduous and steep. Leaders encourage others to continue the quest. They inspire others with courage and hope.
>
> –Jim Kouzes and Barry Posner
> *The Leadership Challenge*

What Intuition and Research Tell Us

It is probably self-evident to you and to most people that a committed, engaged workforce is a productive workforce. And that a productive workforce is critical for an organization to achieve its desired business results.

There is a growing amount of research to back up intuition and personal experience regarding the importance of motivated people at work. Jeffrey Pfeffer, for example, in his book *The Human Equation: Building Profits by Putting People First*[1], provides impressive evidence, analysis, and real-life examples proving a correlation between good people management and profits. He found out that returns from managing people in ways that build high commitment, involvement, learning, and organizational competence are typically on the order of 30 to 50 percent. Such returns are substantial by any measure.

Based on additional research, Pfeffer, joined by co-author Charles O' Reilly, in their book, *Hidden Value*: *How Great Companies Achieve Extraordinary Results with Ordinary People*[2], make several conclusions regarding good people management. They include:

- Organizations that manage the human factor well offer their employees more than a job. They offer a sense of community, security, and mutual trust and respect.
- The interest in hiring individual stars is a fad that will pass as companies realize that their success depends on what they do with and to their talent, not just acquiring it.
- Many organizations miss the link living a set of values and creating the alignment between values and people and place too much emphasis on strategy and not enough on values and the management practices that produce implementation.
- Decades of research has documented how increased monitoring can undermine motivation and cause previously engaged people to reduce their effort.

A Competitive Advantage

Patrick Lencioni in his book *The Advantage: Why Organizational Health Trumps Everything Else in Business*[3], argues that to be successful organizations need to be both *smart* and *healthy*. Being smart means doing all the traditional organizational functional specialties such as strategy, marketing, finance, and technology well. Being healthy means engaging in good people management practices.

In his work Lencioni finds that even well-informed leaders who see the wisdom in having both a smart and healthy organization will usually focus most of their attention on the smart side of the equation. Why? Even though wise leaders recognize the importance of the healthy side of the equation, they like the smart side because it is more objective and measurable, and they just feel more competent and comfortable in that arena.

Lencioni states that the advantages to be found in the classic areas of business, such as strategy, finance, marketing, and technology, in spite of all the attention they receive are incremental and fleeting. He sees the greatest opportunity for organizational improvement and competitive advantage in organizational health. An organization that is healthy will inevitably get smarter.

I do take exception with Lencioni placing *strategy* under the smart side of the equation. The wise leader formulates and executes strategy to develop *both* a smart and healthy organization.

A Significant and Sad Workplace Gap

Research findings reinforce Lencioni's experience regarding the lack of attention being placed on building healthy organizations.

Gallup's 2022 *State of the American Workplace*[4] reports:

In surveying 195,600 U.S. employees and 31 million in their Q^{12} Client Database, Gallup reports that only:

- 33% of U.S. employees feel engaged at work compared with 70% of employees working for the world's best organizations.
- 21% of employees strongly agree their performance is managed in a way that motivates them to do outstanding work.
- 22% of employees strongly agree the leadership of their organization has a clear direction for the organization.

- 15% of employees strongly agree the leadership of their organization makes them enthusiastic about the future.
- 13% of employees strongly agree the leadership of their organization communicates effectively with the rest of the organization.

So, despite what would appear to be axiomatic to most leaders and backed by solid research results, the vast majority of entities are not engaging in sound people management practices to become healthy organizations.

What is causing this sad workplace phenomenon?
A variety of reasons can be cited:[5]

- Despite the large amount of evidence, many organizational leaders refuse to believe the connection between how organizations manage their people and business results.
- Many executives who see the connection take simplistic, faddish approaches in attempting to grow healthy organizations rather than employing the comprehensive and systematic approaches required, including the training and coaching of leaders throughout the organization on an ongoing basis.
- Long-term thinking is the exception rather than the rule, leading executives to focus mainly on short-term financial results and meeting quarterly numbers.

You as a Leader Can Be a Game Changer

Regardless of your role and level in your organization you can have a strong influence on your leadership playing field in building a healthy work environment.

There have been numerous studies over the years validating the important role the local line leader or immediate supervising manager has on building a committed workforce. One nationwide study involving 1,500 employees discovered that although there are multiple factors affecting employee engagement, the personal relationship between the supervising manger and his or her direct reports is the most influencial.[6]

You as the supervising manager play a pivotal role in your associates' commitment. You serve as the primary conduit connecting your associates to the balance of the organization. You are their voice and echo their needs. They look to you to accurately translate what is going on in the organization as it affects them. They want to have a strong personal relationship with you as their manager and want to know that you care about them and their well-being.

Your attitude and actions as a supervising manager are critical for fostering a culture of commitment. What you do, how you behave, and what you say and how you say it greatly affects your associates' attitudes about their work and the organization as a whole, which in turn can have a significant impact on the bottom line. Research findings over the decades consistently report that the number one reason people choose to stay or opt to leave their organizations is their relationship with their supervising manager. The increasing turnover rates in today's world of work and recruiting costs being approximately 1.5 times annual salary underscore the valuable role you as the supervising manager play relative to the health of your organization.

If you are fortunate to be working in a healthy organization the challenge of fostering a work culture of commitment is going to be a lot easier for you. You have a running head start. But regardless of your organizational context and its health, the concepts, structures, processes, and tools, described in my book, *Making and Fulfilling*

Your Dreams as a Leader, and this book, *Building Commitment*, equip you with the capability to develop a *sound strategy* and *committed people* for you to achieve extraordinary results in your role as a leader. That role being to fulfill the definition of a leader, that is, to mobilize people to struggle for shared aspirations.[7]

2. UNDERSTANDING MOTIVATION: COMMITMENT VERSUS COMPLIANCE

> Perhaps the most promising trend in our thinking about leadership is the conviction that the purposes of the group are best served when the leader helps followers to develop their own initiative, strengthen the use of their own judgment, and enable them to grow and to become better contributors.
>
> –John W. Gardner

Before exploring the four building blocks for fostering a work culture of commitment, let us review what we know about the motivation to work and to perform.

Movement versus Motivation

Let us start with a basic, but vitally important principle. That is, motivation is not something you do to someone. That is movement. True motivation comes from within a person. Motivation is goal-directed behavior intended to satisfy individual needs.

Figure 2.1 Motivation Is Goal-Directed Behavior

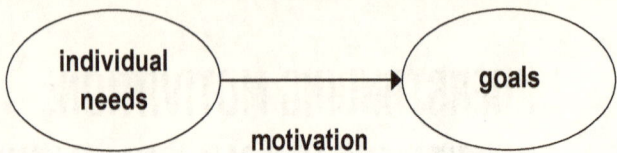

You as a leader do not motivate anyone. Your role as a leader is to build and sustain a motivational environment so that people can get their individual generators spinning. There are of course times you will need to move people, also known as the KITA (kick in the posterior) approach. But the better the environment you set to an get people engaged, the less you will need to use movement.

Your goal as a leader should be to build and sustain a work culture of commitment as contrasted with one of compliance. In a work culture of commitment, people *want to perform*, as contrasted with a work culture of compliance where people feel they *have to perform*.

Figure 2.2 Contrasting Work Cultures

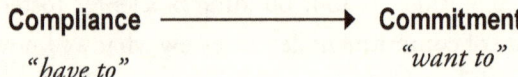

Theories of Motivation

Let us explore two theories of motivation that have been with us for some time, but continue to be critical in helping us understand just what true motivation is.

Maslow's Hierarchy of Needs[1]

Abraham Maslow's *Hierarchy of Needs* goes all the way back to the 1940's. Maslow categorized human needs into five categories and suggested that they could be arranged in a hierarchy as shown below.

Figure 2.3 Maslow's Hierarchy of Needs

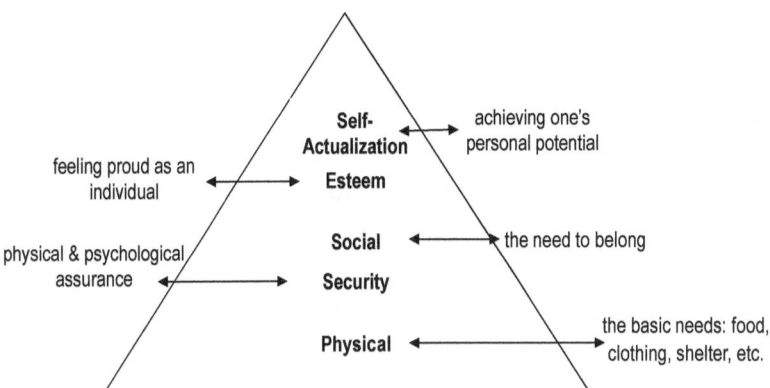

Maslow postulated that once one set of needs was basically fulfilled, although they were still important, it no longer served as a primary motivator. The primary motivator then becomes the next level of needs in the hierarchy. An individual could also move down the hierarchy as well as up. Suddenly being out of work, for example, most likely could heighten the security need for an individual.

Maslow's hierarchy of needs is based primarily on his clinical experience. But he also drew on observations and experiments. His intent was to formulate a positive, holistic theory of human motivation.

As a result of his research, Maslow believed that self-actualization was reserved for a select few. Further research on positive mental health since Maslow's death in 1970 indicates that this need level was a lot more obtainable for people then Maslow thought. It has become increasingly clear that to become more self-actualized, people need to simply get out of their own way and overcome the conditioning they have become accustomed to relative to who they are supposed to be.[2] In addition to what further research has shed on the subject, there is just much more room in today's world of work with the proliferation of what Peter Drucker calls *knowledge work*, as contrasted with *manual work*[3], for people to find avenues to explore their unique destinies. Drucker states that knowledge workers are mobile because they own the means of production. It is the knowledge between their ears.

The challenge for organizations and for you as a leader is to establish and maintain an environment in which individual aspirations and goals can be aligned with organizational identity and direction. That is, individual needs and aspirations are satisfied in pursuit of shared organizational aspirations.

Figure 2.4 Aligning Aspirations and Goals

Individual Aspirations and Goals ⇒ Organizational Identity And Direction

Herzberg's Motivation-Maintenance Theory

Before going into Frederick Herzberg's *Motivation-Maintenance Theory*, also known as the *Two Factor Theory of Motivation*, take a few minutes to work through the exercise below.

EXERCISE: What Turns You On?

What to do

1. Thinking back a year or so at your organizational work experience, answer these two questions:
    a. What specifically ***satisfied** you the most* (that is, "turned you on the most")?
    b. What specifically ***dissatisfied** you the most* (that is, "turned you off the most")?

2. Analyzing your answers to the questions above, was the *most satisfying* thing for you *individual-centered* (that is, *the work itself*—something you specifically did or did not do), or *organization-centered* (that is, *the work context*—the world surrounding your work—the workplace, the way you were treated, organizational policies and practices, and so forth)? How about your *most dissatisfying* thing? Did it come from the work itself or the world surrounding the work (the work context)? Think about it and check your answers below.

	(The Work Itself)	(The Work Context)
The source or origin of my **satisfying experience** was: *(Check the appropriate box to the right)*	☐	☐
The source or origin of my **dissatisfying experience** was: *(Check the appropriate box to the right)*	☐	☐

Herzberg's seminal findings on work motivation grew out of his and his colleagues research in the 1950s and 1960s. His findings as well as Maslow's are, and this bears repeating, still very much relevant today and provide a foundation for our understanding of the nature of work and worker motivation.

The research prior to Herzberg's important research and findings focused on human relations problems within the organization. Herzberg's *The Motivation to Work (1959)*[4] summarized his research. The study showed that people are made *dissatisfied* by a bad environment, the extrinsics of the work. But they are seldom *satisfied* by a good environment, what Herzberg called *hygiene*. Worker *satisfaction* or fulfillment came from achievement and growth derived from the work itself. This was a huge breakthrough.

As the research began to be applied in the years to come, the term *maintenance* began to be used in lieu of hygiene. This is a good term in that organizations need to continually maintain good working environments if they are going to be able to continue to operate. I will use the term maintenance in lieu of hygiene from here on out. But, as the research tells us, a good working environment does not translate into worker motivation. Instead, satisfaction comes most often from factors intrinsic to the work. That is, such things as achievement; earned recognition; and, work that is challenging, interesting, and responsible.

Herzberg's research was based on workers' accounts of real events that made them feel good or bad about their job. The findings refuted the previously held belief that worker satisfaction could be measured on a single scale. What emerged was a two-factor theory of motivation. Some factors were *dissatisfiers* and others were *satisfiers*.

In subsequent research by others, instead of asking workers to describe a "time they felt very good or very bad on the job", as Herzberg and his researchers did, workers were asked to describe "a time they worked very hard or a time they put forth little effort." These studies lent further support to all the evidence that satisfiers are motivators.

Herzberg's book, *Work and the Nature of Man (1966)*[5] and the article "One More Time: How Do You Motivate Employees?" *(1968)*[6] summarized the many replications of the original study. This article is the most reprinted article in the history of the *Harvard Business Review*.

But it took some time for the relevance and the importance of Herzberg's research and findings to catch on. Human relations continued to be the primary worker motivation focus into the 1960s and 1970s.

UNDERSTANDING MOTIVATION: COMMITMENT VERSUS COMPLIANCE

The chart below helps clarify the *Motivation-Maintenance Theory*. The key thing to note is that the opposite of being dissatisfied is not satisfied, but not dissatisfied; and the opposite of being satisfied is being dissatisfied, but not satisfied. Got it? Kind of confusing at first. But once you have it, you really have something.

Figure 2.5 Herzberg's Maintenance-Motivator Theory

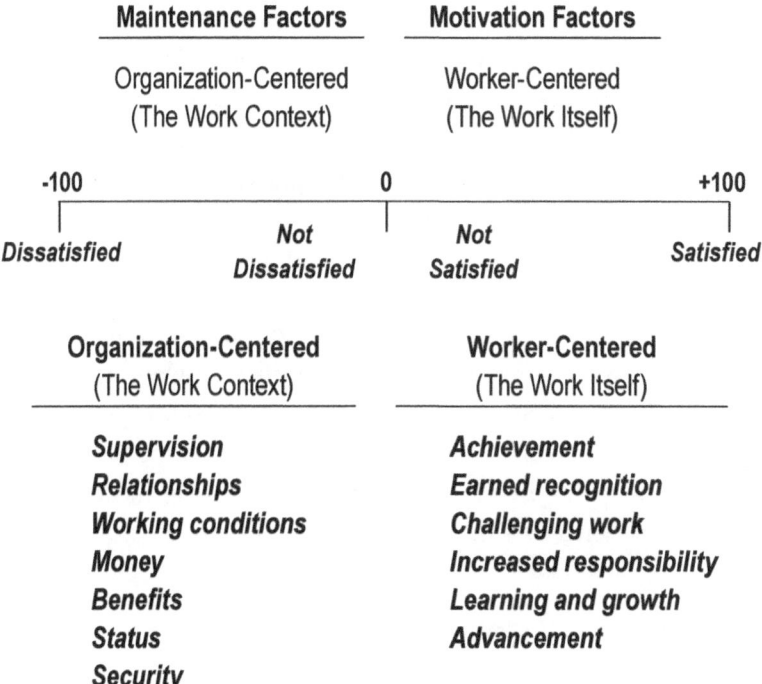

Regarding the money factor, an important thing to understand is that money can be a motivator. But it is not the money itself that motivates. Rather, it is the translation of what the money might mean to the worker. For example, if the perception of the money received is equated with accomplishment and hard work being duly recognized, it can indeed be a motivator. But even when money is a motivator its staying power is short-lived.

A correlation can be made between the earlier work done by Maslow and his *Hierarchy of Needs* and Herzberg's *Motivation-Maintenance Theory*. What have been called the "lower- order needs" in Maslow's hierarchy, that is, the physical, security, and to some extent, the social need level, relate to Herzberg's maintenance factors. And what have been called the "higher-order needs" in Maslow's hierarchy, that is, to some extent the social need level, and most definitely the esteem and self-actualization need levels, relate to Herzberg's motivators.

Herzberg became widely known as the "Father of Job Enrichment". This title sprung from the job design strategy called job enrichment that grew out of the *Motivation-Maintenance Theory*. The idea was to look at the way jobs could be reengineered to provide greater motivational power. We will talk more about this important strategy in Chapter 5, *Performance Coaching: Guiding Success*.

Did the results of the exercise you did earlier in this chapter regarding your most dissatisfying and satisfying work experiences match Herzberg's findings? How about your work experiences in general over the years? As unscientific as it may be, the class profiles of the participants of the many leadership and management seminars I have conducted over the years certainly substantiate the theory.

The Evolution of Management Models

It is both interesting and informative to trace the evolution of management models over time in the United States. Our discussion of work and motivation up to this point in this chapter will help you both understand and appreciate this evolution and its implications.

We draw upon the work of Raymond Miles in taking this journey.[7]

Pre-Industrial Society

In the 1800s the U.S. was an agrarian society. What firms did exist were small and owner-managed. Authority was concentrated in the hands of the owner-manager. Employees were considered as extensions of the owner. They were hired hands, working only for money. Close supervision was seen as essential to assure employees completed their assignments. "When the cat's away, the mice will play."

In the late nineteenth and early twentieth century, a rapidly growing economy spurred dramatic growth in firm size and ushered in the industrial society. And today we have what is referred to as the information society.

The following pages summarize the predominant management models for the various historical periods described. I will use the basic structure Miles used in describing these historical periods, adding my own comments.

The evolution of the various management models did not originate out of the goodness of the hearts of leaders as to how best manage people. Rather, these shifts were business driven. And there is nothing wrong with that. Organizational leaders saw ideas and changes happening in the broader society and adapted accordingly. It is especially interesting to trace the evolution of worker needs in general as described in Maslow's *Hierarchy of Needs* and the shifts in the various management models.

Figure 2.6 The Evolution of Management Models

Traditional Model (1880-1920) ⇨ Human Relations Model (1920-1960) ⇨ Human Resources Model (1960-1990) ⇨ Human Investment Model (1990s→)

Let us now describe each of these historical periods and the management model that evolved.[7]

The Traditional Model

Origin
(1880–1920s)

- More and more people working for firms.
- Firms getting bigger.
- Market size increasing with transportation improvements.
- Workers at the physical and security need levels in Maslow's *Hierarchy of Needs*.

Assumptions

- Work is inherently distasteful to most people.
- What workers do is less important than what they earn for doing it.
- Few want or can handle work which requires creativity, self-direction, or self-control.

Management's Role

- Closely supervise and control people.
- Tasks must be broken down into simple repetitive, easily learned operations. (Application of F.W. Taylor's "Scientific Management".) Reducing tasks to the lowest common denominator eases replacing people and minimizes training requirements.

- Establish detailed work routines and procedures and enforce firmly but fairly.

Expectations

- People can tolerate work if the pay is decent and the boss is fair.
- If tasks are simple enough and people are closely controlled, they will produce up to standard.

The Human Relations Model

Origin
(1920-1960)

- Workers in general evolving to the social need level in Maslow's hierarchy.
- As an outgrowth of Scientific Management, Western Electric conducted a series of studies (1924–1932) at its Hawthorne Works outside of Chicago. The initial study focused on the effects of lighting and productivity. Then other variables such as temperature, piped in music, various compensation schemes, and working hours were studied.

    But regardless of the changes in the physical environment, for example increasing or decreasing lighting, production went up. The researchers were stumped as to why. A group of anthropologists from Harvard University led by Elton Mayo were called in to help find out what was going on. What emerged is that the positive results were due to the social effect. All the changes that were going on were interpreted by workers as a sign that management cared which provided mental stimulation that was good for morale and productivity. In addition, the fact that the groups being studied were separated from the rest and given special treatment developed a certain bond and camaraderie that also increased productivity.

The phenomenon that emerged from these studies is called the Hawthorne Effect.

- It was in the 1930s and 1940s that labor unions gained a foothold in the United States. Labor legislation paved the way. The Norris-LaGuardia Act of 1932 barred the federal courts from issuing injunctions against non-violent labor disputes, and created a positive right of noninterference by employers against workers joining labor unions. The Labor Management Relations Act, comprised of the Wagner Act of 1935 and amended by the Taft-Hartley Act of 1947 defined acceptable and unacceptable labor practices for both management and labor unions as well as establishing dispute resolution processes.

But, once workers were free to vote to be unionized or not, the primary reason that those who voted to be represented did so was not bread and butter issues, but rather *dignity*.

Assumptions

- People want to feel useful and important.
- People desire to belong and to be recognized as individuals.
- These needs are more important than money in motivating people to work.

Management's Role

- The manager's basic task is to make each worker feel useful and important.
- Subordinates need to be informed and listened to.
- Subordinates should be allowed to exercise some self-control on routine matters.

- Suggestion plans, company events, and employee newsletters were born in this era.
- The bottom line was to communicate with employees, treat them well and fairly, and consult them on small matters.

Expectations

- Sharing information with subordinates and involving them in routine decisions will satisfy their need to belong and feel important.
- Satisfying this social need will improve morale and reduce resistance to formal authority.

The Human Resources Model

Origin
(1960-1990)

- Workers moving to the higher-order needs in Maslow's hierarchy.
- Herzberg's *Motivator-Maintenance Theory*, was a key piece of research.
- Douglas McGregor's influential book, *The Human Side of Enterprise*,[8] was a pivotal conceptual piece. McGregor argued that the traditional assumptions, which he called Theory X, represented by the Traditional Model and Human Relations Model discussed, needed to be replaced with a new set of assumptions, which he called Theory Y. Theory Y postulated that workers were willing and able to contribute in significant ways if given a chance.

Assumptions

- Work is not inherently distasteful. People want to contribute to accomplishing meaningful goals which they have helped establish.
- Most people can exercise far more creativity, responsibility, self-direction and self-control than their present jobs demand.

Management's Role

- The manager's key role is to make use of "untapped" human resources.
- An environment needs to be created that allows all members to contribute to the limits of their ability.
- Full participation on important matters needs to be encouraged, continually broadening subordinates' self-direction and control.

Expectations

- Expanding subordinate influence, self-direction, and self-control will lead to direct improvements in operating effectiveness and efficiency.
- Work satisfaction may improve as a byproduct of subordinates making full use of their resources.

The Human Investment Model

Origin
(1990)

- Workers continue to ascend Maslow's hierarchy.
- Global competition. The flat world.
- The impact of the effectiveness of teams and Total Quality Management.

- Technological advances.
- The learning organization.

Assumptions

- Most people can acquire knowledge and skills far beyond current job demands.
- Core competencies can represent a sustainable competitive advantage.

Management's Role

- Invest in education, training, and the development of capability to innovate, grow and learn.

Expectations

- Investment in education and training leads to the ability to creatively adapt and the development of a learning organization.
- Multi-directional communications.
- The lateral organization.
- The growth of teams, both natural work group and ad-hoc.

I hope that this chapter has been both interesting and informative to you. It sets the stage for you to better understand and appreciate the significance of the four building blocks of commitment that we will now proceed to explore.

3. BUILDING BLOCK #1: SELECTION: CHOOSING THE RIGHT PEOPLE

> An organization that wants to build a high spirit of performance recognizes that "people" decisions are the true "control" of an organization.
>
> –Peter F. Drucker

> The most important thing is that the person and the assignment fit each other.
>
> –Peter F. Drucker

People Turn Dreams into Realities

To optimize its effectiveness an organization needs to continuously work toward a clear, sound strategy consisting of a shared identity and direction supported by an aligned and integrated structure and systems. But dreams not supported by actions are just that—dreams. And it is the people that accomplish the necessary actions that determine to what extent the dreams come true.

BUILDING BLOCK #1: SELECTION: CHOOSING THE RIGHT PEOPLE

Staffing is a critical management function.

Staffing: Choosing and equipping people to effectively perform the work necessary to achieve desired results.

Objectives of the Selection Process

The selection process is an accumulation of steps leading to the placement of an individual (or individuals) in a specific position, project, or assignment. In speaking of the selection process, we are referring to both external "hires" and internal "placements".

The objective of the selection process should be to assure a "good fit". That is, the process should lead to a good match between the individual qualifications and interests needed to achieve the desired results and the person chosen for the opportunity.

A poor fit will only lead to difficulties. When a good fit exists adjustments in position responsibilities and authorities can and should be made to allow for the incumbent's learning and growth. But when significant over or under-employment exists, such adjustments are not feasible, resulting in significant performance problems.

Figure 3.1 Assuring a Good Fit

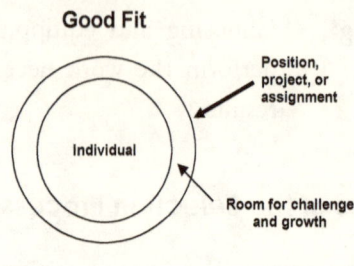

Good Fit
- Position, project, or assignment
- Individual
- Room for challenge and growth

Mismatches

Individual too big for position or assignment — Individual / Position, project, or assignment — Boredom, apathy

Position or assignment too big for individual — Individual / Position, project, or assignment — Overwhelmed

Common Selection Problems

Despite the importance of the selection process, hiring managers have traditionally felt uncomfortable and many do not do well with the process. Not fully appreciating the importance of the process to assure a good cultural, position, and career fit is a partial explanation for this discrepancy. Lack of selection and interviewing skills is also a major factor.

Some of the common problems experienced by interviewers include:

- Not knowing what they are looking for.
- Hiring in their own image.
- Not being organized.
- Lack of adequate preparation.

- Jumping to conclusions.
- Talking too much.
- Inability to obtain any relevant information that is not already on the resume or application.
- Failure to control the interview.
- Not going through a logical decision-making process after completing the interviews.

The following pages show you how to use practical and proven concepts, structures,, practices, processes, and tools to increase your confidence and skill in conducting effective interviews and select the right people to match the opportunities you have available. The methodology described can be used for seeking and selecting candidates for any kind of position. The examples used are slanted toward professional positions. As appropriate, modify the process to fit your specific selection needs.

The Selection Process: The Steps

Whether you are looking inside or outside the organization, or both, to select someone for your opportunity, the recommended steps are the same.

1. Develop a Position Profile.
2. Develop Selection Criteria.
3. Source candidates.
4. Prepare an Interview Guide.
5. Conduct interviews and use other appropriate means for gathering relevant candidate information.
6. Make the decision.

Step 1. Develop a Position Profile

Position Profile: A summary of the primary components of a position, or family of positions, that allow for the identification and definition of individual qualifications needed to be successful in the position.

Figure 3.2 Selection Criteria Developed from Position Profile

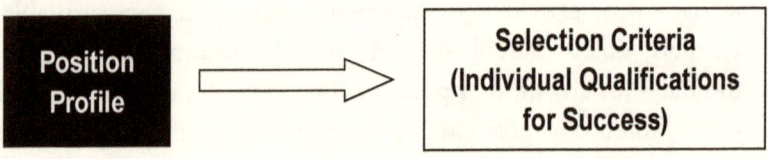

Position Profile Components

Component	Purpose	Benefits
Purpose (Role)	To summarize the reason the position exists.	Provides focus. Answers the fundamental question: "What is the business of this position?"
Key Result Areas (Responsibilities)	To identify the major segments of results. If the position has leadership responsibilities, in addition to the appropriate technical KRAs, a leadership/management KRA needs to be included.	Divides desired results into logical categories to ease specifying desired results and needed qualifications.
Tasks (or Essential Job Functions)	To list the key tasks that the incumbent has to *personally perform.*	Identify the work of the position.
Key Opportunities or Challenges (Goals)	To take a look into the future.	Identify areas for goal setting.
Organizational Culture	To summarize the characteristics of the relevant environment surrounding the position.	The culture as well as position requirements are critical to review in filling vacancies.

Position Profile Example

Position: *Business Unit Compensation and Benefits Manager*   Date Prepared:_____

Purpose:	Coordinate the implementation, changes, and administration of corporate compensation and benefit plans; and, to design special compensation plan, strategies, and practices to fit the unique needs of the business unit when and as needed.
Key Result Areas:	1. Leadership and Management 2. Compensation Planning and Administration 3. Benefits Administration
Tasks:	• Plan and coordinate the section's direction. • Supervise professional and administrative staff (currently 3 people). • Work with corporate compensation group to coordinate roles, strategies, and work. • Work closely with business unit management in developing and implementing appropriate business unit compensation plans to fit business needs. • Direct administration of both corporate and business unit compensation plans. • Direct administration of corporate benefit plans.
Key Opportunities and Challenges:	• Design and implement a performance-based incentive plan for all employees in the business unit that allows all to appropriately share in key business unit performance achievements. • Need to do a comprehensive job evaluation survey to pick up where the corporate survey leaves off. Need to look at industry-specific job matches. Need to work collaboratively on this effort with corporate compensation group. Could be sensitive. Once done, need to institutionalize the results.
Organizational Culture:	Very technical, demanding clients. Fast-pace, rapidly changing environment. Still a heavy "process" culture, but starting to see the need to change in certain areas that do not require detailed procedures and strict adherence to such procedures. Business unit has corporate-wide reputation of being a maverick and provincial.

APPLICATION: Developing a Position Profile

What to Do

1. Select a position to focus on to practice the steps in the selection process. The ideal is a current opportunity you have or anticipate having. If you do not have a current opportunity, select another position you are familiar with. If all else fails, use your own position.

2. Recreate the Position Profile Worksheet shown below and draft a Position Profile.

POSITION PROFILE WORKSHEET

Position: _____ Date: _____

Purpose (or Role): *(A single sentence summary of why the position exists or is being created)*

Key Result Areas: *(Logical subdivision of position responsibilities. Use just a word or two for a label. If it is a managerial position, include "Leadership and Management" as a Key Result Area.)*

-
-
-

-
-
-

Tasks: *(Key activities the person needs to perform.)*

**Key Opportunities
And Challenges:** *(Key goals)*

**Organizational
Culture:** *(Describe the culture)*

Step 2. Develop Selection Criteria

Purpose

A well-crafted Position Profile provides the necessary focus to develop Selection Criteria. *Your selection needs to be based not on the Position Profile, but rather on the Selection Criteria you derive from a careful review of the Position Profile.* Your Selection Criteria represent the requisite individual qualifications needed for a person to successfully achieve the desired results for the position and operate in the organizational environment, as summarized by the Position Profile.

Selection Criteria Components

General Qualifications	A general description of qualifications required, including any position-relevant education and experience, and any needed or desired certifications or registrations.
Position Success Factors	The critical few attributes needed for a person to be successful in the position.

General Qualifications

The general qualifications are useful to get the word out in sourcing candidates. That is. letting people know of the opportunity through internal and external notification practices, such as postings, advertising, working with recruiters, word of mouth, and so forth.

General qualifications also serve as a useful initial screen to make "go/no go" decisions regarding candidates interested in the position. How well a person meets the general qualifications can for the most part be obtained from a resume or application. But general qualifications should be used for screening and not making your selection decision. To increase your rate of hitting bull's eye in selecting the right people you need to do the required quality thinking necessary to identify and define a meaningful list of Position Success Factors (PSFs) and then use them to steer your selection process and decision-making.

Types of Position Success Factors

One of the important decisions you as a hiring manager need to make is just how much time and effort you are willing to devote to developing a person to succeed in the opportunity you have available. Do you want or need a person to "hit the ground running"; or, is it more advantageous to select a person who has what it takes but needs some development?

The graphic below is useful in both helping you to think about the different types of PSFs as well as the developmental difficulty associated with each type of PSF.[1]

BUILDING COMMITMENT

Figure 3.3 Types of Position Success Factors

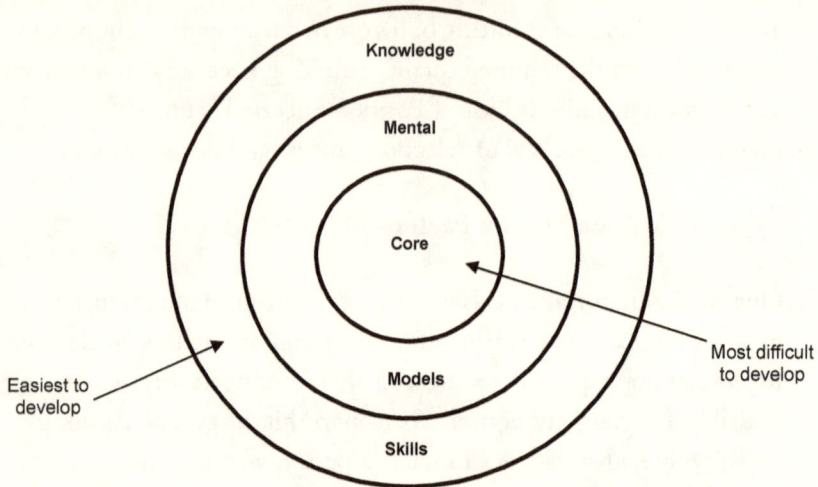

Core	A person's innermost self—talents or abilities, traits, physical characteristics, subconscious priorities and preferences, motives, mood.
	Examples: analytical ability; need for affiliation; "big picture thinker"; calm under pressure; visual preference for receiving and giving information; etc.
Mental Models	A person's assumptions, values, beliefs acquired or developed as he or she has experienced life.
	Examples: Honesty; integrity; trusting of others; respect for authority; balanced life style, etc.
Knowledge and Skill	Knowledge: Information a person possesses in specific content areas.
	Examples: Plant operations; technical savvy; and so forth.
	Skill: competence to perform a specific physical or mental task.
	Examples: Critical thinking; public presentations; determining cause and effect relationships; etc.

Selection Criteria Example

Listed below are the General Qualifications and Position Success Factors that were developed from the Position Profile for the position shown earlier.

Position: Business Unit Compensation and Benefits Director

General Qualifications:

- Prior comprehensive compensation experience is a must. Would like to see at least 5 years.
- American Compensation Association certification desirable.
- BA/BS degree. MBA preferred.
- Familiarity with databases.

Position Success Factors:

- Compensation Acumen
- Directing Others
- Project Management
- Quantitative Analysis
- Collaboration
- Influence
- Motivation

Identifying Position Success Factors (PSFs)

Use the following categories to help you identify the critical few PSFs for the position you are focusing on.

<u>Technical Work</u>

What are the essential knowledge and skills needed to perform the technical work of the position? Technical work being defined as the direct application of physical and mental effort to produce the products and services of the position.

Determine if you want to consider the Technical Work as a whole as a PSF, or to subdivide into a few critical elements. In the example above of a Compensation and Benefits Director, the Technical Work PSF was subdivided into two critical elements: Compensation Acumen, and Quantitative Analysis.

Leadership and Management

If the position includes a leadership role, include Leadership and Management as a PSF. Management Work being defined as coordinating and directing day-to-day activities to achieve desired results. Leadership is about charting a future and executing strategies to achieve it.

Just as with the Technical Work PSF, consider Leadership and Management as a whole to be the PSF, or subdivide it into the few critical elements. In the Compensation and Benefits Director example above, the Leadership and Management PSF was subdivided into Directing Others and Project Management.

Personal Characteristics

In addition to any technical and leadership/ management requisite knowledge and skills, consider any personal characteristics that are critical to success in the position.

In doing so, you are delving into the core and mental models dimensions of the Types of Personal Success Factors model shown if Figure 3.3 above. Take a look at the examples shown for each of these dimensions in the example to help you understand the kinds of personal characteristics you may want to consider as PSFs.

Motivation

Motivation (or Passion if you prefer) should be an automatic PSF for any position. Just how much is the individual excited about the opportunity? This is critical. We are not talking about pay, benefits, and physical niceties here. These can be important considerations for a candidate. But rather, we are talking about how excited the individual is about your organization's identity and direction and making significant contributions to it. Equally important is how well you see the candidate working effectively with you and your team.

The key questions from the candidate's point of view should be:

- *"Is there a compelling purpose for me that I want to contribute to?"* and,
- *"How well can I work with these people?"*

Peter Thiel[2], who has built multiple breakthrough companies, argues that these two questions are especially important when it comes to talented people. They do not have to work for you. They have options. There is nothing wrong with having a chance to own valuable stock, work with smart people, or to work on important challenges. But such things do not differentiate your organization. Your identity, direction, and culture does.

Potential

Depending on whether or not you think it important that whomever you select can grow in the position and perhaps move beyond your current opportunity, you may want to also include Potential as a PSF. You of course will need to have an idea of what you mean by potential. Especially for professional positions it is useful to think of potential as the capability to adapt to ever-changing business environments and grow into challenging new roles.[3]

APPLICATION: Developing Selection Criteria

What to Do

Using the Position Profile you developed earlier in this chapter for the position you are focusing on, recreate the Selection Criteria Worksheet shown below on a piece of paper and:

- Define the General Qualifications for the position.
- Identify the Position Success Factors.

Developing Selection Criteria Worksheet

Position: _____ Date: _____

General Qualifications *(A general description of qualifications, including any position-relevant education and experience required as well as any certifications needed or desired.)*

Position Success Factors

-

-

-

-

-

-

-

- **Motivation**

Defining Position Success Factors

After identifying Position Success Factors, the next step is to define them. The definition step provides needed clarity by translating the PSFs labels into specific behavioral terms. The definition step is designed to answer the question: *"How do you know success when you see it?"*

The fable below makes the case for this needed clarity when it comes to clearly understanding the required individual qualifications.

A Fable[4]

"Once upon a time in the land of Fuzz, King Ailing called in his cousin Ding and commanded, "Go ye out into all of Fuzzland and find me the goodest of men, whom I shall reward for his goodness."

"But how will I know one when I see one?" asked the Fuzzy.

"Why, he will be *sincere*," scoffed the king, and whacked off a leg for his impertinence.

So, the Fuzzy limped out to find a good man. But soon he returned, confused and empty-handed.

"But how will I know one when I see one?" he asked again.

"Why, he will be *dedicated*," grumbled the king, and whacked off another leg for his impertinence.

So the Fuzzy hobbled away once more to look for the goodest of men. But again he returned, confused and empty-handed.

"But how will I know one when I see one"? he pleaded.

"Why, he will have *internalized his growing awareness*," fumed the king, and whacked off another leg for his impertinence.

> So the Fuzzy, now on his last leg, hopped out to continue his search. In time, he returned with the wisest, most sincere, and dedicated Fuzzy in all of Fuzzland, and stood him before the king.
>
> "Why, this man won't do at all," roared the king. He is much too thin to suit me." Whereupon, he whacked off the last leg of the Fuzzy, who fell to the floor with a squishy thump.
>
> The moral of this fable is that...*if you can't tell one when you see one, you may wind up without a leg to stand on.*

The format used in defining Position Success Factors includes a definition and behavioral indicators for each identified PSF. The definition defines the PSF in operational terms. The behavioral indicators represent evidences or examples of desirable behavior. The definition and behavioral indicators allow for needed clarity regarding each of the PSFs.

Examples

The following excerpts are used for example purposes only. They are samples drawn from actual applications of PSF profiling. The complete set of PSFs is not shown.

BUILDING BLOCK #1: SELECTION: CHOOSING THE RIGHT PEOPLE

Success Factor	Definition	Behavioral Indicators

Examples for a Territory Manager:

Success Factor	Definition	Behavioral Indicators
Flexibility	Adaptive and receptive to the changing priorities of the business and the varying personalities of individuals.	• Switches to different approaches as conditions change. • Quickly reorganizes own schedule or activities in response to business needs. • Adjusts quickly to new procedures or ways of doing things.
Self-Confidence	Demonstrating self-assurance in unfamiliar or stressful situations.	• Exercises independent judgment about what is right or best. • Demonstrates self-assurance in the presence or senior management.

BUILDING COMMITMENT

Success Factor	Definition	Behavioral Indicators

Examples for District Manager:

Building Agreement	Uses collaborative approaches to build support for objectives.	• Involves others early in the process to gain ownership, support, and cooperation. • Continues to keep people informed in order to maintain their support. • Works for mutually acceptable solutions that benefit all relevant parties.
Customer Focus	Recognizes that the organization's success depends on providing valued service to our diverse customers.	• Listens to and fully understands the customer's needs. • Interacts in an effective and positive manner with customers. • Considers the customer's perspective in making decisions. • Considers consequences to the customer before taking action. • Ensures that commitments to customers are met.

Examples for an officer of a large organization:

Focus on Results	Monitoring progress and holding oneself and others accountable for performance.	• Actively evaluates information on how the unit and its people are doing with respect to goals. • Sets priorities with the right sense of urgency and importance. • Delegates implementation of details and gives direct reports the latitude to decide how the details are best carried out. • Rewards people when they have done well and confronts people directly when they do not demonstrate desired performance.

BUILDING COMMITMENT

APPLICATION: Defining Position Success Factors

What to Do

Continuing to use the position you are focusing on in this chapter for application purposes, recreate the Defining Position Success Factors Worksheet shown below on a piece of paper to define the PSFs you have identified for the position you are working on.

Defining Position Success Factors Worksheet

Position: _____

PSF	**Definition**	**Behavioral Examples**

BUILDING BLOCK #1: SELECTION: CHOOSING THE RIGHT PEOPLE

PSF	Definition	Behavioral Examples

Step 3. Source Candidates

Sourcing candidates has to do with getting the word out, be it an internal search, external search, or both, by using appropriate means and processes. The means and processes are dependent upon organizational practices, the type of opportunity you have, and the supply of suitable candidates. Doing the quality thinking relative to the first two steps just described in the selection process allows you to optimize your sourcing options.

The Selection Interview

Before moving to Step 4 in the selection process, Prepare an Interview Guide, let us discuss some important aspects of the selection interview.

The general qualifications serve as a means for sourcing and screening potential candidates.

Your decision is made via the selection interview and whatever other appropriate supplemental selection mechanisms you might use, such as references, background checks, and so forth.

The PSFs provide the building blocks for developing an interviewing strategy, structure, and making the selection decision.

The purpose of the selection interview is to get to know the real person in the context of the organizational opportunity. The goal is to get to know the person's talents, traits, passions, knowledge, skills, and motivation as they relate to the specific qualifications needed to be successful in the position. It is helpful to think of the selection process as exploring a relationship to see if a *good fit* exists for both parties.

The Unskilled and the Skilled Interviewer

The *unskilled interviewer*, not knowing how to properly prepare for and conduct a selection interview, will tend to talk too much. The interviewer will often go on at length about the organization, the position opportunity, and such things as current organization events, the organization chart, benefit plans, and perhaps talk about him or herself.

The questions the unskilled interviewer asks often have no specific purpose. Sometimes the interviewer will search for a cleaver or trick question, use "pet" questions, or questions usurped from some how-to interviewing book. The problem is that these kinds of questions are not designed to solicit relevant information in the context of the PSFs. The sad part of all this is that most times the unskilled interviewer has little more relevant information about the candidate after the interview than what was already known via the resume or application.

The *skilled interviewer* on the other hand, knows what she is looking for, and prepares accordingly. There is less pressure in the interview to be quick on one's feet and think of questions because the interviewer has a focus and a map. The focus is the PSFs, and the map is an Interview Guide prepared from the PSFs. We will discuss the Interview Guide in just a bit.

Process and Structure

The specifics of the interview process will vary from organization to organization and from manager to manager, and be largely dependent on the opportunity available.

One important dynamic that needs to be given serious consideration is who in addition to the selection decision maker, if anyone, should interview or spend some time with the candidates.

If more than one interviewer is involved in interviewing, dividing the PSFs up among the interviewers is a highly recommended practice. This allows each interviewer to go more into depth on the specific factor or factors he has been assigned. This practice also eliminates the redundancy problem that candidates have to endure when faced with multiple interviewers.

When the interviews are completed, the interviewers use the specific PSFs assigned in discussing the candidate or candidates.

When you involve others in the selection interviewing process, you need to give quality thought ahead of time as to just how the selection decision is to be made. That is, is a consultative or consensus mode of decision-making going to be used? If you do involve others, it is critical that you are genuine in wanting to involve them. You involve others not to make them feel good. You involve them because you value their input in helping to make an informed decision. In addition, when done correctly, their involvement should lead to increased buy-in regarding the decision. In the consultative mode you are genuinely involving others in the interviewing process, but you make the final decision. In the consensus mode, the other interviewers join you in making a decision. You need to decide what mode will work best for you in any given selection opportunity. In any event, the interviewers should be apprised of the decision-making mode in advance. Regardless of the decision-making mode you choose, the Decision-Making Matrix discussed later in this chapter as a part of Step 6 of the selection process provides a useful structure for bringing the interviewers together to discuss their respective interviews and for making a decision.

To allow the final candidates to get a good "feel" for the organization, it is a good practice to allow them to talk to various people in the organization with whom they would be working if selected. The people the candidates talk to should know specifically what their roles are and what is expected of them. And, of course, they should be asked for their feedback and thanked after talking to the candidates. The selection interviewing process may entail more than one visit on the part of a candidate or candidate.

Suggested Interview Structure

Below is a suggested selection interview structure that serves as a guide. Obviously, modify the guide to fit the design of the interviewing process and your preferences and needs.

Stage	Notes	% of Time
Set the climate	• Introductions • Establish rapport • *Overview* of the opportunity. Keep it brief. • Review the interviewing process.	10%
Explore candidate's qualifications and interest	Use Interview Guide prepared in advance to guide interview and take notes.	70%
Allow candidate to ask questions	• The kinds of things a candidate asks you are many times more valuable in making a "position fit" assessment than what you ask the candidate. • Provides opportunity to explore areas not covered that are important to the candidate.	15%
Wrap up	Review next steps	5%

Immediately after the interview, review the notes you made in the Interview Guide (the next topic) for clarity and completeness. Make additions or modifications as necessary.

Step 4. Prepare an Interview Guide

Benefits

Preparing an Interview Guide to be used in conducting your selection interviews with each of the finalists is an extremely practical and proven means for assuring a successful interview.

Preparing and using an Interview Guide allows you to:

- Develop patterns of inquiry and specific questions that logically flow and achieve the objective of eliciting relevant and useful information.

- Assure consistency of interviews in gathering relevant information.

- Arrange for a nice balance of structure and flexibility.

How to Prepare an Interview Guide

Prepare an Interview Guide for each of the candidates you will be interviewing using the steps listed below.

1. Set up a page for the General Qualifications and *each* of the Position Success Factors you have identified.

    Determine if there is a logical sequence or flow for the PSFs and arrange them accordingly in your Guide.

    Place the "Motivation" PSF last in your sequence of PSFs. Typically, by the time you get to Motivation, if placed last in your sequence, you will have already gained quite a bit of useful information and insight and will not have to spend much time, if any, on this specific PSF.

BUILDING BLOCK #1: SELECTION: CHOOSING THE RIGHT PEOPLE

2. If your PSFs vary in importance, now is the time to consider weighing them. Doing so will help you gauge the design and use of your Interview Guide, and how much time to spend on the various PSFs. The weighting can also come into play later on when you conduct your decision analysis using the Decision-Matrix structure described below.

    Recommend using a scale of 1 to10. Assign a weight of 10 to the PSF or PSFs you (or the group if you are working collectively) think is the most important. Assign a weight of from 1 to 9 to the remaining PSFs based on their relative importance compared to the PSF or PSFs you gave a 10 to. The same weighing can be given to more than one PSF.

3. On the top of each page, write down the questions you want to ask or situations you wish to pose for the General Qualifications page and each of the PSFs. Recommendations for developing questions and situations and how to ask or pose them are described below.

    You only need a few questions or situations for each PSF. You do not need to use them all in the interview. You will be asking additional clarifying or guiding questions of the candidate based on the flow of the interview and his specific responses to your prepared questions.

    The balance of the page is used for your note taking.

    Explain to each candidate that you have prepared a guide to help make the most of the interview, and that you will be taking notes throughout the interview to help you remember the conversation.

    Be skillful in taking notes. Make them brief, and try not to let your note taking interfere with the flow of conversation.

Step 5. Conduct Interviews and Use Other Appropriate Mean for Gathering Relevant Candidate information

Guidelines for Constructing Impactful Inquiries

The Guiding Principle

Remember that your goal is to have the real person emerge in the interview. Given that a person's past interests, behavior, performance, and motivation are good predictors of future interests, behavior, performance, and motivation, you want to construct relevant lines of inquiry that will require a person to describe *what they actually did or would do and their thinking or feeling driving such behaviors.*

Specific Guidelines

- Make your questions simple, direct, and specific.

- Avoid cute, trick, or "pressure cooker" questions.

- Make sure there is a positive and valid intent to each of your lines of inquiry and specific questions.

- *Limit your talking to asking the questions* and posing the situations you have in your Interview Guide and relevant follow-on inquiries.

  (Remember that your main focus in the interview is to seek to understand what the candidate is really saying and not saying so that you can make effective assessments. Given that you have already done your homework in advance, effective listening will be a lot easier than it otherwise would be.)

- *Use "open-ended" questions* as contrasted with "close-ended" questions.

  (Closed-ended questions can be answered by a "yes" or "no", or by a word or two. For example, "Do you consider yourself to be a good delegator?" Open-ended questions, on the other hand, require some elaboration. For example, "How do you go about determining just what should be delegated; and how do you go about making the delegation?")

- Consider using *"tell me about" questions* for starting to probe into General Qualifications and for transitioning into new topics during the course of the interview.

  (For example: "Tell me about your marketing role at Acme Enterprises".

  "Tell me about your experiences at Purdue University.")

- Use *inquiry* questions to probe into areas you want to explore further.

  (For example: "You said you particularly enjoyed the design work you did at Rolly Enterprises. What is it about design work, or the particular design work you did there, that excites you?")

- Consider using some *third-party questions* during your interview.

  (For example: "What is it about you that motivated the homeowners to appoint you as President?"

  "If I were to ask your former boss Sam about you, what would he say?")

- In discussing success stories, be sure to ask the candidate what he specifically did to help achieve the success.

  Otherwise, you may end up discussing the challenge, the work, and the overall results, and never find out just what the candidate's role was, and just what she did, thought, or felt.

- In that past behavior is most times a good predictor of future behavior, *behavior questioning* is encouraged. But in using behavior questioning you want to avoid using loaded words such as adapt, successfully, balance, and persuade. You also want to avoid using leading phrases such as "tell me how you did it" and stick more to open-ended questions such as "so what happened next" so that candidates will feel comfortable telling you that they took no action.

Some examples:

ORIGINAL: Tell me about a time when you adapted to a difficult situation and how did you do it.

IMPROVED: Tell me about a time you faced a difficult situation.

ORIGINAL: Tell me about a time when you had to successfully balance competing priorities.

IMPROVED: Tell me about a time you faced competing priorities.[5]

After the candidate has responded to your neutral questions to start a topic, such as the IMPROVED statements above, you can then use behavior questions to dig into areas you wish to pursue by asking a series of behavior questions.

For example:

> "What was going through your mind?"
>
> "How did you react?"
>
> "What was your rationale?"
>
> "Would you handle the situation the same way if you were able to replay it?
>
> "What, if anything would do different?"
>
> "What did you learn from this experience?"

Here are some additional examples of behavioral interviewing:

Position Success Factor	Possible Questions
Results Orientation	"Have you been involved in a business or product launch?"
	"What was your role?"
	"Tell me about how you handled the role"
	"What were the results?"
Team-Centered Leadership	"Describe a time you were asked to lead a challenging team project."
	"How did you go about it?"
	"What were some of the major obstacles you encountered?"
	"How did you react?"
Strategic Thinker	"What are the top three strategic challenges or opportunities your current organization faces?"
	"How would you address these challenges or opportunities?"
Change Agent	"Describe a time you received substantial organizational resistance to an idea or project you were responsible for implementing."
	"How did you handle it?"
	"What were the results?"
	"What did you learn?"

- Use position-related or task-relevant *situational questions* to probe into important topics.

    (Allows you to hear or see how the candidate might react to relevant situations that did or could happen.)

    For example: "Barbara, we had a critical incident come up last month. I'd like to describe the situation to you, and have you tell me how you would have handled it, and why.")

- If at all possible, have the candidate *demonstrate performance.*

    (Sometimes this can happen just in the course of an interview. For example, if "Interpersonal Skills" were a PSF, you could assess this factor in the interview. But most times, you have to be a little bit more creative. Perhaps there is a task you could have the candidate perform during or after the interview. Or perhaps you could give an assignment. Sometimes it may even be feasible for a candidate to "try on" the opportunity for a short stint.)

APPLICATION: Constructing Inquiries

What to Do

Continuing to use the position you are working on throughout this chapter for application purposes, recreate the structure below on a piece of paper and write down an impactful line of inquiry, that is, a few specific questions or situations you would pose, for a couple of PSFs to hopefully have the true candidate emerge. As described earlier, when designing a full Interview Guide, devote a separate page for each PSF with your few questions or situations for each PSF shown on the top of the page and leaving the balance of the page blank for your note taking during and after the interview.

BUILDING BLOCK #1: SELECTION: CHOOSING THE RIGHT PEOPLE

Constructing Inquiries Worksheet

Position Success Factor: _____

Position Success Factor: _____

Step 6. Make the Decision

Decision Matrix

The decision matrix structure is ideal for making your selection decision. You can use it by yourself or working collectively with a group. As with any tool used for engaging in deliberative analysis, it needs to support, not supplant, your intuitive sense. *The decision matrix shown is quite rigorous. Feel free to modify it to fit your needs.*

Figure 3.4 Decision Matrix

Decision Matrix Candidates

Position Success Factors	Wt. (1-10)	A Sc. (1-10)	Wt. Sc.	B Sc. (1-10)	Wt. Sc.	C Sc. (1-10)	Wt. Sc.	D Sc. (1-10)	Wt. Sc.	E Sc. (1-10)	Wt. Sc
•											
•											
•											
•											
•											
Totals:			___		___		___		___		___

Scoring your decision matrix is shown on the following page.

Scoring

Weighting PSFs   Recommended weighting each of your PSFs earlier when we were discussing *Preparing an Interview Guide*. Weighting helps you plan for the interview and better allocate your interview time, spending more time on the more important PSFs. Now, if you wish, you can use your weights to help you make your selection decision.

Rating Candidates   Regardless of whether or not you factor in the weights you may have assigned to each of your PSFs, you will want to rate each of the candidates interviewed. To do so, recommend again a 1-10 scale with the candidate that you rate tops for a specific PSF getting score of 10. The balance of the candidate scores for a specific PSF are the then compared to the candidate who scored a 10. You can give the same weighting to more than one candidate. Every candidate must however be given at least a score of 1.

Weighted Score   The weighted score for each candidate is the weight (if you use them) for each PSF x the Score you give the candidate for the specific PSF.

Totals   Totals are derived by summing up each of the weighted score columns or, if you did not factor in weights, the Score columns, for each of the candidates.

As mentioned above, if the decision matrix structure as illustrated is too rigorous for you, modify it to fit your needs.

If you make modifications, continue to use the KSFs you have identified and defined to assess each of the candidates for the position.

Below are some of the modifications you may want to consider to make the structure as shown less rigorous.

Weighing the PSFs

- Do not weight the PSFs if you consider them to be of relatively equal importance.

- Or, if just one or two PSFs are deemed to be important, assign a value to only that PSF, or those PSFs, rather than to all the PSFs. For example, rather than assign a 1 to 10 weight for each PSF, you could give extra weight to a specific PSF by assigning it a multiplier factor, for example 1.5x or 2.0x. Then you would multiply each candidate's score for that specific PSF by the multiplier.

Individual Scoring

- Assign individual scores based on how well you think the candidate meets the specific PSF, rather than on how well the candidate stacks up to the other candidates.

- Simplify the scoring by using a 1 to 5 scale rather than 1 to 10 scale. Again, 1 being the lowest score.

Integrated Thinking

Your decision matrix is a valuable tool. It allows you to quantify your decision making in comparing candidates.

But in using such a rigorous and structured process such as a decision matrix it is worthwhile taking one additional step in making your final decision. That step involves reflective thinking about how comfortable you are with the decision indicated by your decision matrix.

A Right Brain Check

The decision matrix definitely involves left brain, linear, methodical, analytical, rational thinking. You want to now use some right brain, conceptual, intuitive, creative thinking to arrive at an integrated decision.

What do your gut instincts tell you about your rational decision arrived at through your decision matrix? Are your rational, left brain, and intuitive, right brain, thinking in sync?

Adverse Consequences

A second check on your tentative decision is to think through any potential adverse consequences regarding the decision. This check is particularly valuable when the totals for two or more candidates are closely bunched in your rational decision-making.

Ask yourself such questions as:

> *"How will this decision hold up over time?"*
>
> *"Will it be a good selection in the face of changing conditions?"*
>
> *"Are there any crucial factors I have overlooked?"*

For any adverse consequence identified, ask yourself:

> *"What is the **probability** of this consequence occurring; and,*
>
> *"If it does occur, what is the **seriousness**?"*

4. BUILDING BLOCK #2: CLARITY: DEVELOPING SHARED EXPECTATIONS

> The first responsibility of a leader is to define reality. The last is to say thank you. In between the leader is a servant.
>
> –Max de Pree
> *Leadership Is an Art*

> Tell me what you want, not what you want me to do.
>
> –Source unknown

Assuming you planned and conducted a selection interview as outlined in the previous chapter, you have already discussed important organizational and position challenges with your new associate as well as many important expectations. Now it is time to be more explicit in developing shared expectations. This chapter will help you to engage in quality dialogues at the outset of the relationship and on a continuing basis to develop, monitor, and modify both ongoing and time-limited shared expectations.

Organizational Clarity

It is important that your new associate, or any associate, understands the organizational context within which you work. The organizational context is the organization as a whole, and a department, division, business unit, line of business, that you may align with in optimizing your ongoing decision-making and contributions.

The *Strategic Framework* model shown on the following page, and which I describe in detail in my book, *Making and Fulfilling Your Dreams as a Leader: A Practical Guide for Formulating and Executing Strategy*[1] provides the structure for having a quality dialogue regarding your organizational context.

Figure 4.1 Strategic Framework

IDENTITY	DIRECTION
(Core ideologies) *"Who we are"* *"What we stand for"*	(Stimulating progress) *"Where are we going?"* *"What it looks like when we get there?"* *"How we're going to get there?"*
Purpose Why we exist. What our business is. **Core Values** Our essential and enduring beliefs based on key business ideas that guide our everyday thinking, behavior, and decision-making. **Distinguishing Features or Capabilities** Unique characteristics that allow us to create value for our customers.	**Vision** An ideal and unique image of the future for the common good. **Strategic Path** Our approach to achieving our Vision. The critical few strategic thrusts (strategies, goals, or initiatives) that will propel us toward achieving our Vision. **Actions** Specific things we need to do to accomplish each of our strategic initiatives.

Position Clarity

This chapter describes three practices that are invaluable for you to develop both ongoing and time-limited shared expectations with each of your associates. The three practices are position planning, goal setting, and action planning.

Crafting a Position Plan[2]

You of course do not stop at just providing organizational clarity. You need to also assure a shared understanding of the role and responsibilities of your associate's position.

Traditional job definitions, born largely out of labor-management contracts, do not do the trick. Job definitions are designed to draw boundaries around jobs. Job descriptions do not do the job either. Job descriptions typically list the activities rather than results to be performed by a box on an organization chart, often including the dubious "and perform other duties as assigned" statement.

What does do the trick for assuring understanding of specific role and responsibilities is a *Position Plan*.

Position Plan:	A living, working document that defines the purpose and ongoing set of results a position, or family of positions, and those reporting to the position, if anyone, are organized to achieve.

The position plan provides an ideal framework in today's fast-paced, ever-changing world of work for *agreeing on results, not activities.* The position plan is not meant to be a finalized or perfect product. Rather, it serves as a living, working document for you and your associate, or family of associates, to agree on shared expectations regarding both current and emerging realities. The primary benefit of utilizing the position planning logic is not the document itself, which is extremely valuable, but the quality thinking and interacting the planning logic evokes between you and your associate.

The position planning logic helps develop accountability. Accountability is a sense of ownership or stewardship to achieve desired results. A person's commitment increases when there is clarity regarding what is expected, a belief that what one is doing is important, and making significant contributions to make it happen.

Accountability: The obligation to *achieve specific results*.

Responsibility: The obligation to *perform specific tasks (activities)*.

In addition to achieving position clarity, there are several other significant benefits that can be derived from applying the position planning logic.

Figure 4.2 The Position Plan: Foundation for an Integrated Performance Management System

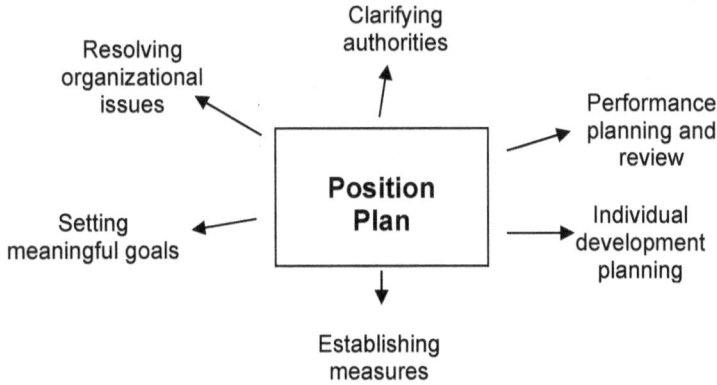

Issue Bin

Invariably, as you apply the position planning logic, questions and issues arise regarding roles, responsibilities, and authorities. This is the position planning logic doing its job. The large share of such issues typically are boundary management questions.

As such issues arise, do not fret. Again, this is just the position planning logic working for you. Make note of such issues on a sheet of paper, labeled *Issue Bin* or *Parking Lot*.

At some point you will want to get back to your issue bin and work on resolving the issues you have made note of. In doing so, ask the following questions:

- Is the issue worth resolving?
- Do I have the authority or influence to resolve the issue?
- Can the issue be resolved on the spot?
- If the issue cannot be resolved on the spot, what is the prudent action to be taken to resolve the issue?

Reflect the resolution of issues that emerge in the position plan, or in the case of boundary management issues, position plans.

The model below depicts the position plan structure.

On the following pages the position plan components are discussed.

Figure 4.3 Position Plan Structure

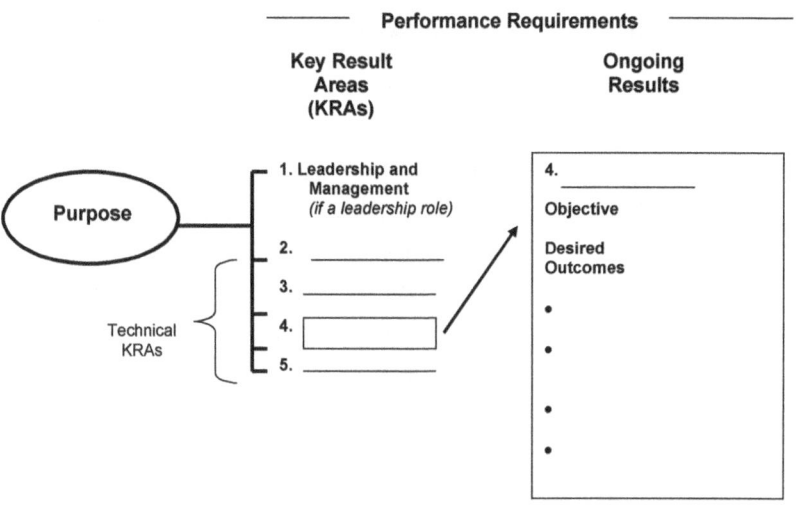

Crafting a Purpose Statement

Purpose: The reason a position and those reporting to it exists.

Defining Purpose would seem to be quite simple and straightforward. But, "what is our business?", be it for the organization as a whole, an organizational unit, or a position, is almost always a difficult question, and the right answer is usually anything but obvious.

> I find certain images about common purpose very powerful. If you believe deep down that you and the others you work with have common purposes and values, you can still certainly pursue different objectives. Inevitably people will have different goals. But, if I really can believe deep down that, in spite of those practical differences, we still have an enormous amount in common that we actually care

about, then that changes my whole view. In that case I start to see myself and others less as separate beings, and more as parts of a greater whole.

–Peter Senge

Defining the purpose of the business (or position) is difficult, painful, and risky. But it alone enables a business (or position) to set objectives, to develop strategies, to concentrate its resources and go to work. It alone enables a business (or position) to be managed for performance.

–Peter F. Drucker

Guidelines for Drafting a Purpose Statement

- Limit to one sentence.

- Define from the customers', clients', or users' point of view. It should be stated as a *result*. That is, *"what the customers find, or could find, of value or worth"* (The Value Proposition). Purpose needs to capture the *why* of a position; not *what* it does, or *how* it does it. It is okay, in fact many times desirable, to briefly summarize what a position does, and maybe how it does it in a purpose statement as long as the result of the activity, that is the why, is stated.

- The purpose should be far-reaching and timeless. The purpose should be broad enough so as not to restrict quality thinking regarding strategic direction in alignment with the organization's essence; but specific enough to provide meaningful direction.

- Need to be able to feel some passion about the purpose.

Some Examples of Purpose Statements from Position Plans

Director of Facilities, children and family center:

> Provide safe, clean facilities for children, families, and staff that support their quality of life and enhance the effectiveness of the agency's work.

Director, Information Systems Engineering, bank:

> Help the enterprise better serve our customers and be more productive and profitable by providing technology solutions and access to information.

Family of Inspector positions, municipal water treatment facility:

> Assure that the general public, industrial, commercial, and residential customers understand and accept their responsibilities related to maintaining water quality and behave accordingly.

Construction Superintendent, water district

> Install assigned planned improvements and perform emergency repair is a safe, cost-effective manner to ensure quality, reliable, and economic water services for the district's customers.

> Until thought is linked with purpose, there is no intelligent accomplishment.

> –James Allen

BUILDING COMMITMENT

Application: Crafting a Purpose Statement

Remember that defining purpose is not easy. You will want to reflect on it and come back to it several times until you are satisfied. You will also want to get constructive input from constituents.

Follow the process described below to draft the purpose statement for the position you are working on.

I. Answer the following questions:
   a. Who are the position's primary customers, clients, or users?
   b. What do the customers/clients/users find, or could find, of value or worth)?
   c. If you think it makes for a more meaningful purpose statement, go ahead and include a brief summary of what the position does, and perhaps how it does it, if doing so enhances the meaningfulness of the purpose statement. But do so only after you have properly answered the two questions above.

II. After you have answered the questions above to your satisfaction, pull the elements together to form a well-worded, powerful one-sentence summary that captures the essence of the position.

III. Test your draft by asking yourself the following questions:
   - Does the purpose statement summarize what the customers, clients, or users find, or could find, of value or worth?
   - Is the purpose statement far-reaching and timeless?
   - Does the purpose statement provoke "a fire in the belly"? How about at least a little tingle? If not, we have a problem.

Developing Performance Requirements

There are two steps in developing performance requirements:

1. Identify the position's *Key Result Areas*.

2. Define the *Ongoing Results* to be achieved for each *Key Result Area*.

    - Define the ongoing *Objective* for each of the Key Result Area.
    - Define the ongoing *Desired Outcomes* that taken collectively represent the conditions that exist when the Objective is being achieved.

1. Identifying Key Result Areas

Key Result Areas (KRAs): Logical groupings or areas of accountability.

Key Result Areas (KRAs) serve as the building blocks for thinking about, talking about, and defining ongoing expectations.

A position typically has from two to six Key Result Areas (KRAs). A listing of over six areas is an indication that perhaps you may not be doing enough logical clustering of result areas. Or, perhaps activities, as contrasted with results, are distorting your thinking. Remember, a distinguishing feature and value of the performance planning logic is that, unlike the arcane job description, it focuses on results, not activities.

Label for each KRA. Limit to a word or few words.

If the position has a leadership role, one KRA should be: "Leadership and Management". The balance of the KRAs will be logical groupings of technical work. If the incumbent of the position you are working on has a leadership role, it may be that she actually performs very little technical work in some or all of the technical work KRAs. But nevertheless, that person is still accountable for achieving the position's desired results. And that is exactly what we are trying to do with the Position Plan—define accountability in terms of specific results, not responsibility by listing activities.

The Rationale for Including Leadership and Management as a KRA

When you think about it, leadership and management can be thought of as overhead work. Meaning, that this critical work does not directly produce any bottom-line results for the organization. It is be nice to think that people could just be set free to do their thing and the organization could do good things. But that is totally unrealistic. For without the requisite identity and direction provided by leadership, and the coordination provided by management work, ineffective and inefficient work performance would abound.

So, given the vital nature of leadership and management to organization success, it is critical that an organization in general, and a supervising manager specifically, define leadership and management expectations.

Defining leadership and management expectations allows the organization and the supervising manager to:

- Assure consistency of desired leadership and management behaviors.

- Place people in leadership positions based on assessing the full requirements of the position, and not basing decisions primarily on technical acumen.

- Logically develop the requisite leadership and management capabilities.

- Offset the natural tendency for most people to want to perform technical work over leadership and management work. There are a host of reasons for this *Principle of Technical Priority*. These reasons include: the tangibility of the technical work; the comfort and satisfaction derived from performing the technical work; the rewards and recognition that typically ensue from being a technical expert; the fear of becoming technically obsolete; and, lacking the clarity, confidence, and competence to perform leadership and management work. This *Principle of Technical Priority* is particularly acute in frontline management positions where all of a sudden the person is expected to perform leadership and management work as well as technical work. Developing shared leadership and management expectations is a crucial step to offset this technical priority principle. Managers need to make managers manage. They have to make the performance of leadership and management work matter. And managers need to be provided timely and effective training and coaching to allow them to succeed.

Examples of Key Result Areas

Listed below are some examples of KRAs from various position plans.

Director of Facilities:
1. Leadership and Management
2. Work Request Reception and Resolution
3. Maintenance Management Program
4. Safety and Emergency Response

Director, Information Systems Engineering:

1. Leadership and Management
2. Project Management
3. Account Management
4. Infrastructure Design and Maintenance
5. Application Integration
6. Regulatory Compliance

Producer, Audio-Visual/Video Services (not a leadership position):

1. Consulting
2. Video Production
3. Video Direction
4. Script Writing/Design

Division Manager:

1. Leadership and Management
2. Marketing
3. Engineering
4. Manufacturing

Customer Services Supervisor:

1. Leadership and Management
2. Customer Inquiries
3. New Business
4. Credit and Collections

Inspector family of positions (not leadership positions):

1. Permitting Process
2. Inspections
3. Compliance
4. Public Education

Maintenance Superintendent

1. Leadership and Management
2. Facilities Maintenance
3. Safety and Security
4. Electrical Engineering

2. *Defining Ongoing Results*

There are two steps in defining Ongoing Expectations:

a. Crafting an Objective for each Key Result Area.

b. Crafting Desired Outcomes for each Objective.

> *a. Crafting an Objective for Each Key Result Area (KRA)*
>
> The objective summarizes the ongoing result to be achieved for a specific KRA.
>
> In that some, if not many, of the KRAs may represent intra-organizational work that must be coordinated and performed to effectively serve the position's customers, there may be a need to speak to "what is provided", that is, a summary of products or services, as well as "how it is provided". This is okay. But do not lose sight of who the beneficiaries and the value they receive or could be receive.
>
> Constantly identifying the customer and assuring that there is a value proposition from the customer's point of view is the antidote for bureaucracy creep. Bureaucracy is the hallmark of a self-serving organization. A bureaucracy is an organization that has lost sight of who its customers are or should be. Not being clear about just who the customers are, or failing to acknowledge this critical relationship, leads to assessing what needs to be done and how with only an internal standard in mind.

Examples of Objectives

The following examples are samplings from various position plans.

Operations Supervisor:

1. Work Request Reception and Resolution

> Objective
>
> Establish and maintain a process and staff capability that ensures that all work requests, regardless of how received, are immediately documented in a standard format, prioritized, scheduled, and worked to ensure effective resolution.

2. Maintenance Management Program

> Objective
>
> Maintain and administer the computerized maintenance management program to ensure that routine equipment maintenance actions are performed in a timely and effective manner.

Director, Information Systems Engineering

1. Infrastructure Design and Maintenance

> Objective
>
> Build and maintain the systems infrastructure to provide high reliability and performance for the enterprise.

2. Application Integration

> Objective
>
> Build, install, or manage installation of systems created in-house or by third parties so that the finished product meets our standards and provides expected levels of service to users.

Inspector family of positions (not a leadership position):

1. Permitting Process

> Objective
>
> Assure that industrial customers understand the applicable environmental requirements related to their business and what they need to do to meet those requirements.

2. Inspections

> Objective
>
> Have inspections at industrial and commercial facilities performed with the intent being that they are informative and instructive to assure compliance with discharge requirements.

3. Compliance

> Objective
>
> Assure that when corrective action is needed compliance is achieved by providing appropriate

>   information to the customer and using a cooperative effort to achieve long-term solutions.
>
> 4. Public Education
>
>   Objective
>
>   Provide timely and relevant information and help to all customers to develop an understanding and acceptance of responsibilities in monitoring and maintaining water quality.
>
> Maintenance Superintendent
>
> 5. Safety and Security
>
>   Objective
>
>   Assure that effective safety and security programs exist and protect employees and the District's customers.

Defining the Objective for the Leadership and Management KRA

For a leadership position, the definitions of leadership and management work, provide the basis for defining an objective for the Leadership and Management KRA.

> Leadership: The art of mobilizing people to want to struggle for shared aspirations.[3]
>
> Management: Coordinating diverse activities to achieve desired results.

For frontline managerial positions, where a lot more management work than leadership is typically performed, the definition of management work may serve well as the Objective.

For example, the Objective for a frontline management position might read:

1. Leadership and Management

    Objective

    Coordinate the diverse activities of the work group to achieve desired results.

For a higher-level position that has a substantial amount of both leadership and management, a blend of the two definitions would work well.

For example:

1. Leadership and Management

    Objective

    Set a direction that optimizes and mobilizes effort to achieve shared aspirations; and provide the necessary coordination of diverse activities to make it happen.

Obviously, feel free to use your own wording to tailor the objective to your expectations of the position.

b. *Defining Desired Outcomes for Each Objective*

Desired Outcomes are the success criteria for the objective. They answer the question:

"How do you know success when you see it?"

Desired Outcomes are expressions of evidences of desired results. They are conditions that exist *when* the objective is achieved. They are expressed in the present tense.

Examples of Desired Outcomes

Continuing with some of the examples of KRAs and resultant objectives shown above, below are some examples of desired outcomes.

Director, Information Systems Engineering

1. Infrastructure Design and Maintenance

    Objective

    Build and maintain the systems infrastructure to provide high reliability and performance for the enterprise.

    Desired Outcomes

    - Systems infrastructure has sufficient capacity, does not have any performance bottlenecks and uses current technology.

    - Systems are available when expected and users are aware of planned outages and status of problems.

- New systems and business areas can be integrated without major redesign of infrastructure components.

- Systems infrastructure issues never hold up a business decision.

Inspector

1. Permitting Process

Objective

Assure that industrial customers understand the applicable environmental requirements related to their business and what they need to do to meet those requirements.

Desired Outcomes

- Appropriate categorical pollutant limits are set.

- Cooperative working relationships are developed with customers to achieve compliance. Such cooperative efforts include providing relevant technical information and problem-solving inspections. The intent of establishing and maintaining such cooperative relationships is to achieve compliance with permitted objectives while minimizing enforcement.

- Required permitted information is included within the permit. Such permitted information is consistent with applicable federal and state requirements.

- The brokering process as it relates to significant industrial users is explained and understood. The major users understand which pollutants are available for brokering, when it is appropriate to make adjustment to their permits, and how to make such adjustments.

- Appropriate sampling locations for required monitoring or self-monitoring are identified and established. Customers understand their self-monitoring and tracking process responsibilities and meet such requirements. Customers are

- Customers understand what pretreatment removal equipment is required and their responsibilities to ensure that the equipment functions properly at all times. Frequency of customer contact assures that appropriate corrective action is taken in a timely manner.

Maintenance Superintendent

1. Safety and Security

    Objective

    Ensure that effective safety and security programs exist and protect employees and the District's customers.

    Desired Outcomes

    - The Safety committee works in an effective manner to truly make the District a safe place to work.

    The Committee accomplishes its purpose and safety results by:

    - Providing and using an upward line of communications from employees to management.

BUILDING BLOCK #2: CLARITY: DEVELOPING SHARED EXPECTATIONS

- Reviewing safety performance and incidents to identify appropriate corrective actions and improvements to be implemented.
- Fostering District-wide ownership for achieving desired safety results.
- Incenting ongoing safety improvements and results.

- OSHA compliance is maintained to ensure that standard work practices are implemented and followed. Such compliance is achieved through audits and resultant implementation of improvement plans.

- Common expectations for department-specific safety training are defined, understood, and accepted. The requisite time, funding, and instructional resources are provided to ensure the desired results are achieved.

- A system exists to ensure that required safety-related equipment is identified, obtained, and kept in reliable working condition so that such equipment effectively serves the purpose for which it is intended when it is needed. Proper inventory management and identification and procurement of new equipment needed to comply with district safe work practices and local standards and authorities ensure the ongoing viability of the system.

- A Security Plan exists that allows the district to mitigate threats pursuant to the vulnerability assessment. The plan serves as a means to promote workforce awareness and establish and use best practices for personal, facility, equipment, and customer security.

Example of Ongoing Results for a Leadership and Management KRA

This example is from a mid-level management position.

1. Leadership and Management

   Objective

   Develop and sustain a viable shared strategic direction and coordinate the diverse activities necessary to effectively and efficiently meet current and anticipated department needs.

   Desired Outcomes

   - Quality strategic thinking occurs on an ongoing basis to allow the department to move forward. Innovations and improvements the department can make to effectively enhance its contribution to the department's success are identified and implemented. The department's strategic plan consists of a continuous mix of a few critical goals and resultant action plans that guide the department in achieving these innovations and improvements and propelling it in the desired direction.

   - Appropriate planning tools are used to effectively plan, schedule, and perform recurring maintenance work and integrate non-recurring work.

   - As needed, work is coordinated with other departments to properly integrate work efforts and increase overall productivity by helping each other out.

   - Work is assigned to optimize the availability of personnel and to match the knowledge and skills with the work to be done. Exceptions to this principle are made to provide needed development of people to perform certain kinds of work or specific tasks.

- People are selected to fill regular or temporary positions and opportunities based on the requisite knowledge and skills needed to be successful in the position and an assessment of the individuals' capability and commitment to learn, grow, and assume greater responsibilities.

- Timely and effective coaching, training, and "hands on" experience is provided to ensure continuous development of people in the ranks for their specific classifications and to prepare them for advancement.

- Proper and timely planning and necessary developmental strategies and actions optimize effective succession for all positions.

Goal Analysis[4]

Defining Desired Outcomes is an ideal application of Goal Analysis. The Goal Analysis tool is a practical and proven way to move from abstract to more specific language. You do so by focusing on your objective or goal and citing specific evidences of success through your Desired Outcomes statements. In other words: "How do you know success when you see it?"

> **Goal Analysis:** A procedure to analyze a goal (or objective) to specify evidences, that is, desired outcomes, success criteria, behaviors, and so forth that, if achieved, would cause you to say that the goal was successfully met.
>
> Goal Analysis is used to help answer the question: "How do you know success when you see it?"

The Steps

1. Write down the **GOAL** (in this application the Objective of the KRA being defined).

2. **JOT** down in words and phrases the evidences that, if achieved, would cause you to say that the goal was successful met.

3. **SORT** out the jottings into logical categories or clusters.

4. **LABEL** each cluster. Develop a "header" (just a word or two) for each cluster that summarizes the cluster.

5. **EXPAND** each label into a statement that captures the essence of the ideas expressed in the cluster, i.e., the jottings. Mentally preface each statement with the word "when", in that the statements represent the conditions that exist *when* the goal (Objective) is achieved.

6. **TEST** the list of criteria. "If all of these criteria were being met, would I say the goal was being successful met?" If the answer is "no", determine what is missing. If the answer is "yes", your goal analysis is complete.

Figure 4.4 Position Plan Format

The format shown below is for putting your Position Plan together.

Date each page. Remember, the intent is to have the Performance Plan serve as a living, working document. When the document needs to be refreshed due to penciled notes, modifications, coffee stains, and a crumpled look, do so.

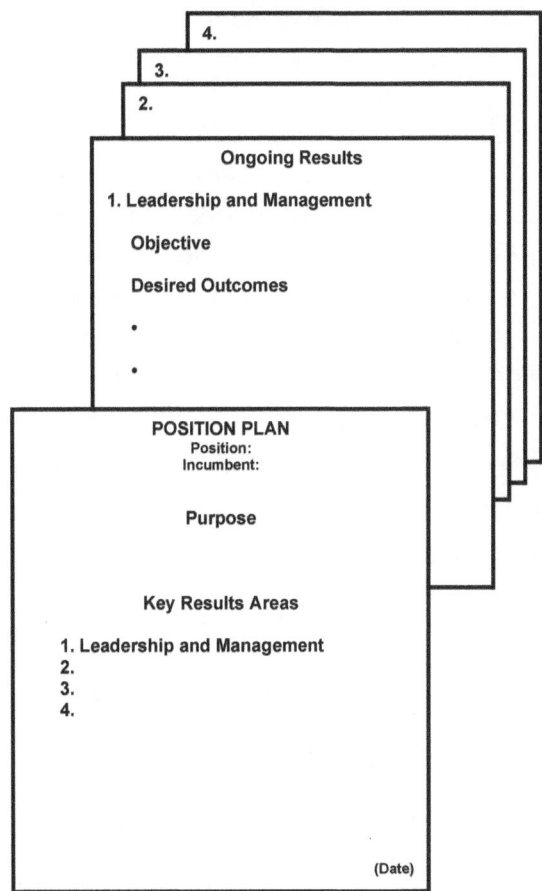

In getting started with the quality thinking needed to draft a meaningful Position Plan, you may decide to initially just "frame out" the plan. That is, begin with just a draft Purpose and KRAs. Doing just this can pay huge dividends. Studies have shown that when paired comparisons are made when supervising managers and associates independently draft KRAs, or the equivalent, and then compare their lists, substantial and critical differences often exist.

In doing the quality thinking necessary to draft the Performance Requirements, you may want to, if you deem it appropriate, collaborate with the current or pending incumbent of the position in drafting the objective and desired outcomes for each KRA.

You may even think it desirable for your associate to draft the performance requirements, once you have agreed on the purpose and KRAs of the position. The draft provides a focus for a constructive performance coaching session or series of sessions. Before using this approach, you of course will need to educate your associate in the position planning logic. And, believe that your associate has enough position-relevant knowledge to prepare a workable draft that would not require major reediting. A major rewrite on your part could be demoralizing.

Setting Meaningful Goals

Whereas the position planning logic provides you with a practical and proven structure to define *the role and ongoing set of results* a position and those reporting to it, if any, is organized to achieve, goal setting focuses on identifying the *time-limited results* to be achieved.

Goal: A targeted desired result.

Goals are not fantasies, wishes, or dreams such as "to make a difference", "to improve the performance of the department", and so forth. Rather, goals are clear, specific written expressions of intent. You may want to improve your department, but to be a goal you need to summarize in a sentence not only your intent of improving the department, but specifically how you plan to do so, and by when. For example: "Improve the effectiveness and efficiency of tracking our client medical records by designing and implementing an appropriate technical solution to move from manual to automated tracking by August, 20xx."

At times you may not know specifically how you are going to achieve your intent. On such occasions, specify the path you are going to take to identify the appropriate solution. In the example above, if the goal setter did not know that "moving from manual to automated tracking" was going to be the specific solution, she would include in her goal the path she planned to take to discover the proper solution. Perhaps she would use wording such as "by identifying and implementing appropriate improvement strategies."

To summarize, a goal is a one-sentence of:

- *What* the desired result is;
- *How* it is going to be achieved; and,
- *When* it is going to be achieved.

The terms *goal* and *objective* are often used interchangeably. Many, if not most, times making a distinction between the two terms is academic. But, when there are several separate but related initiatives required to implement a desired future state, the distinction becomes important. In such cases, I recommend using "goal" to describe the overarching summary of what is to be achieved. And, "objective" to summarize an initiative that is subordinate to the goal. Therefore, when a goal calls for several objectives and resultant action plans to successfully achieve it, this distinction becomes anything but academic.

The Power of Goals

Goals provide a focus, a sense of direction. As such, they catalyze taking positive action to achieve desired results and taking advantage of opportunities that present themselves. The absence of clear, meaningful goals, leads to aimless drifting and merely reacting to one's relevant environment rather than being proactive to move things to new and better places.

BUILDING COMMITMENT

> If you don't know where you're going, you're liable to end up somewhere else, and not even know it.
>
> –Robert F. Mager

> If you don't know where you're going, any old road will get you there.
>
> –Will Rogers

Despite the well-chronicled power of goals, why is it that more businesses and people have not formed the habit of setting clear, meaningful goals?

The reasons include that they:

- Think goals are not important.
- Do not know how to go about setting goals.
- Have a fear of failure.
- Have a fear of rejection.[5]

One of the amazing things about crafting clear, meaningful goals is that you do not have to achieve them to have them start to go to work for you. It is true that if logical actions can be identified and implemented to achieve a goal, the chances of success will be increased. But the very act of formulating a clear, meaningful goal in and of itself catalyzes movement in the desired direction. Goals create a "creative tension" between current realities and desired futures. This creative tension creates the desire to move toward the goal. By setting a goal that is important to you, you begin to pay attention to it and performance in that area starts to improve.

BUILDING BLOCK #2: CLARITY: DEVELOPING SHARED EXPECTATIONS

The Genesis of Goals

It is important that goals be aligned with organizational direction, be it the organization as a whole or one's specific organizational unit. If a position plan exists, it serves as an excellent means of identifying opportunities or challenges worth focusing on.

The well-managed organization effectively aligns, integrates, and coordinates goal setting across and down through the organization to assure that its identity and direction are successfully achieved.

Figure 4.5 Hierarchy of Goals

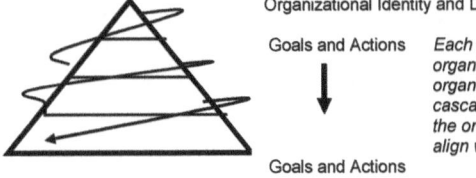

Organizational Identity and Direction

Goals and Actions

Goals and Actions

Each successive organizational level and organizational unit translates the organization's identity and direction as it is cascaded down through the organization to determine how they can best align with and support the overall strategy.

The Number of Goals

The number of business goals for any particular planning period should be held to a minimum. What you want are a few powerful goals that really lead you somewhere. Concentrate on the critical few versus the trivial many (Pareto's Law, also known as the 80/20 Rule, or the Law of the Chosen Few).

Keeping the number of goals to a maximum of five for any particular planning period is a good rule of thumb. The goal mix needs to be a focus of attention throughout the planning period. When a goal is achieved, celebrate and determine if it is appropriate to add another goal to the mix. If a goal is no longer relevant, drop it. Emerging business opportunities or challenges may precipitate the need to set new goals and postpone or drop some other goals currently in the mix.

BUILDING COMMITMENT

If you have a need to prioritize because you have more than enough goal candidates to choose from, *impact, urgency,* and *ease of implementation* serve as practical and proven criteria for doing so. You can assess each of your goal candidates against these criteria in helping you pare down your list. If desirable, you can set up a matrix using a scale let's say of 1 to 5, with 1 being the lowest score, and 5 being the highest.

Categories of Goals

The categories of goals shown below can be useful in helping you choose amongst goals. The categorization looks at the various areas of benefit when it comes to goals.

Figure 4.6 Categories of Goals

Category	Description	
Maintenance	Goals set for major ongoing activities to assure that they are completed.	
Problem Solving	Goals intended to correct deviations from norm, that is, to bring a current result up to standard.	⎯⎯∨⎯⎯
Continuous Improvement	Goals intended to spur steady progress in an important area.	⟶
Innovative	Goals intended to create breakthroughs or radical or discontinuous change that have the potential for resulting in significant improvements.	⎯⎯⎽⌐⎯⟶

Maintenance and problem-solving goals are all about providing continuity, or to correct deviations from norm. Continuous improvement and innovative goals are all about moving things forward. Continuous improvement and innovative goals are your value-adding goals. But obviously, it does not make sense to focus on continuous improvement or innovative goals if a great deal of attention is currently needed on ongoing operational results and activities. You need to walk before you run.

In addition to the categories of business goals as described above, there are also *personal development goals*. The purpose of a personal development goal is to identify and define a timely and unique opportunity or challenge to work on what will foster an individual's learning and growth. Such goals should enhance the performer's capability to make meaningful contributions toward both ongoing and time-limited desired organizational results as well as create a sense of fulfillment for the individual. As with business goals, the focus should be on the critical few and not the trivial many. One or two important personal development goals at any one time are plenty for a healthy growth diet.

Characteristics of Effective Goals

The characteristics of good goals are that they need to be:

- A key business opportunity or challenge.
- Challenging, yet realistic.
- Something that evokes personal commitment and passion on the part of the owner or champion of the goal.
- Clear, specific, and measurable.
- Time-specific.

Setting Realistic Deadlines

In setting deadlines for goal achievement be realistic. Deadlines most times are best guess estimates as to when a goal will be achieved. If a goal is not achieved by the deadline, set another deadline. The more you develop the practice and discipline of working toward realistic deadlines the better you will become in setting realistic timetables for your goals.

The Care and Feeding of Goals

Goals need to be cared for and fed on a regular basis. Manager-associate one-on-one meetings are a great way to assure that there are regular care and feeding schedules for goals. This should not be too difficult. After all, the goals are supposed to represent critical areas of focus and effort. So, talking about them and monitoring and, as necessary, modifying work in progress should be one of the most important things the manager-associate team does as it works together through the course of the year.

"What managers inspect, managers expect" is an old management adage that is oh so true.

So, care for and feed those goals, or shoot them; but do not let them starve to death.

Action Planning

Action Plan:	A process for logically defining, communicating, and implementing a course of action to effectively achieve a goal or complete a project.

Action Plans Need to Be Scalable

The magnitude and complexity of the goal or objective to be achieved should dictate the rigor of the action or project plan required. Although the rational steps for effectively thinking through an action plan, as described in the following pages, are consistent, the comprehensiveness and specificity of the plan needs to vary to fit the application. One size does not fit all.

The degree of rigor required for some action plans are simple enough that the steps can be well thought through in one's head, or scribbled on a notepad. On the other end of the spectrum are project plans needed for large, complex projects that call for a planning team, and maybe even a planning room for crafting, posting, monitoring, and modifying the plan. Examples of the latter would include constructing a power plant or planning for an automobile changeover. Most action planning requirements for managers and associates lie somewhere in between these two extremes.

But regardless of the rigor of the plan required, the steps described here will equip you to logically craft viable action plans.

Go Slow to Go Fast

Quality thinking and interacting at the outset of crafting an action plan can result in huge payoffs during the execution of the work and the accomplishment of desired results. Implementation will go a lot faster and smoother with shared expectations, increased stakeholder understanding and commitment, and a well-thought-out map by which to monitor and modify work in progress in accomplishing the desired results.

Figure 4.7 Total Project Completion Time

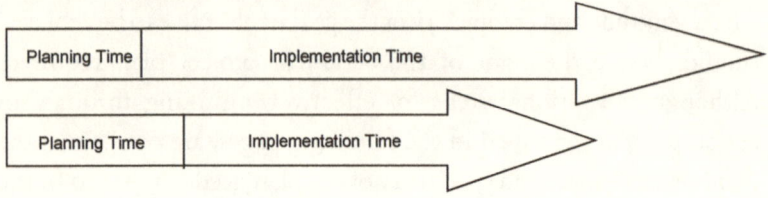

Steps in Crafting an Action (or Project) Plan

Use the steps below to craft viable action plans.

1. **Project Specifications:** Defining Success

2. **Implementation Considerations:** What Lies Ahead?

3. **Work Breakdown Structure:** Identifying the Work Packages and Related Tasks

4. **Work Plan:** Sequencing and Detailing the Work to Be Done

The project specifications defines the *whats* of the project. The work breakdown structure and the work plan lay out the *hows*.

Now let us go through each of the steps and provide you with practical and proven concepts, structures, processes, practices, and tools to allow you to craft viable action plans.

Remember, as discussed above, action plans should be scalable. That is, the rigor required to plan and implement the project should match the project's magnitude and complexity. With simpler projects you can quickly go through each of the steps, or even skip steps (but not the project specification step). With your bigger and more complex projects you will want to rigorously apply each of the project steps.

1. Project Specifications: Defining Success

Defining project specifications, that is, what does success look like, at the outset of a project is crucial. Too often, due to lack of awareness of the importance of specifications, or how to go about defining them, and a rush to get started with the work, this important step is skipped or not given the attention it deserves.

The structure for defining project specifications is shown below.

Summarize the Business Opportunity or Challenge
Why this project?
Why now?

State the Project Objective
What are we trying to achieve?
Summarize the desired result in a well-worded sentence.

Define Desired Outcomes

What does success look like?

The Goal Analysis tool described earlier in this chapter for defining desired outcomes for the various key result areas related to position planning is equally applicable for defining desired outcomes for project success. It can be employed successfully to stimulate and order individual quality thinking or to facilitate quality thinking and interaction with a group of stakeholders.

Describe the Value

What is the value to the organization if we achieved the desired outcomes?

Summarize the value.

Later on in the project planning process, once you have detailed a work plan, you can do a cost-benefit analysis to see just how the time and costs associated with carrying out the project stacks up against the foreseen value.

Summarize Key Roles and Authorities

It makes good sense to define key roles and authorities at the outset of the project before issues and disputes arise and to allow for smoother decision-making.

Briefly describe who is accountable and responsible for what and what their respective authorities are.

The distinction between *accountability* and *responsibility* is an important one when it comes to project planning.

> **Accountability:** The obligation to achieve specific *results*.
> **Responsibility:** The obligation to perform specific *work*.

A project manager, for example, may be accountable for the overall success of the project but not personally perform a great deal of the work on the project. Others are responsible for doing so.

Time Limit

What are the anticipated beginning and ending dates for the project?

An example of a Project Specification is shown on the following page.

Example of a Project Specification
Facilities Group of a Nationwide Organization

Project Plan
Project Specifications

Business Opportunity or Challenge

A comprehensive, nationwide strategy for our facility operations does not exist. Such a strategy would assure that all facilities are operated and maintained in a cost-effective manner, allowing business units to effectively and efficiently achieve their desired results.

Objective

Develop and implement a comprehensive strategy to enhance excellence in ongoing facility operations across the nation.

Desired Outcomes

- Ongoing business unit needs are identified and met or exceeded. Such needs include lease agreements, relocations, and operational requirements.
- Cost effectiveness is achieved by leveraging national contracts.
- Documented facility operational plans are used as an effective vehicle to continuously identify cost efficiencies and areas for improvement. Such plans are developed and maintained in collaboration with the various business units.
- The facilities group results and reputation cause business units to increasingly turn to us to address emerging needs and solve issues and concerns that arise.

Value

Implementation will result in increased operational efficiency and significant cost savings.

Summary of Roles and Authorities

The VP Facilities has overall accountability for the success of the project.

The Midwest Facilities Manager will serve as project manager and make proper use of corporate resources in planning and implementing the work that needs to be done to assure the success of the project.

The COO will serve as project sponsor in support of the project team.

Timing: Start: 4/20xx
Completion: 10/20xx

Date prepared: 3/19/20xx

2. Implementation Challenges: What Lies Ahead?

Where You Are

You have thought through what success looks like for a project by crafting project specifications. You are now ready to plot out the work that needs to be done in the form of a work breakdown structure and resultant work plan to propel you toward achieving success.

But before moving on to specify the work to be done to achieve project success, it is advantageous to look down the road to be traveled to get a good feel for what lies ahead, that is, implementation challenges.

Three tools are described below to help you to look ahead before plotting out specific travel plans.

The three tools discussed below are:

- Stakeholder Analysis
- Force Field Analysis
- Risk Management

Again, as is the case with the entire project planning process, the rigor with which you apply these tools is scalable. That is, your application will be governed by the importance and complexity of the project you are working on.

Stakeholder Analysis

A stakeholder is any person, group, or organization that has a direct or indirect stake in your project because of the effect the implementation of the project will have on the individual or group. The number and type of important stakeholders you will have for any particular project will vary, as will the potential impact each stakeholder or stakeholder group may have on the success of your project.

So before detailing the work needed to be done for the success of your project, it is critical to identify key stakeholders; the potential impact they may have on the success of your project; and, ways to manage these important relationships.

The key stakeholder analysis map shown below is a useful structure for identifying key stakeholders and the potential impact they may have relating to any specific project you are planning.

Position your key stakeholders on your map according to your perception of their receptivity toward the project and their power, both position and personal, to impact it. Your perception of both of these dimensions will most likely change as you manage the relationships at the outset of the project and during the life of the project. But your map will help you plan your strategies as to who you need to engage at the front end of the project, and throughout the life of the project.

An example of a key stakeholder analysis map is shown below.

Figure 4.8 Example; Key Stakeholder Action Map

Project Objective: Refocus efforts to keep continuous improvement efforts moving forward in the division to keep momentum and continue to enjoy the successful results the initiative has given us thus far..

BUILDING BLOCK #2: CLARITY: DEVELOPING SHARED EXPECTATIONS

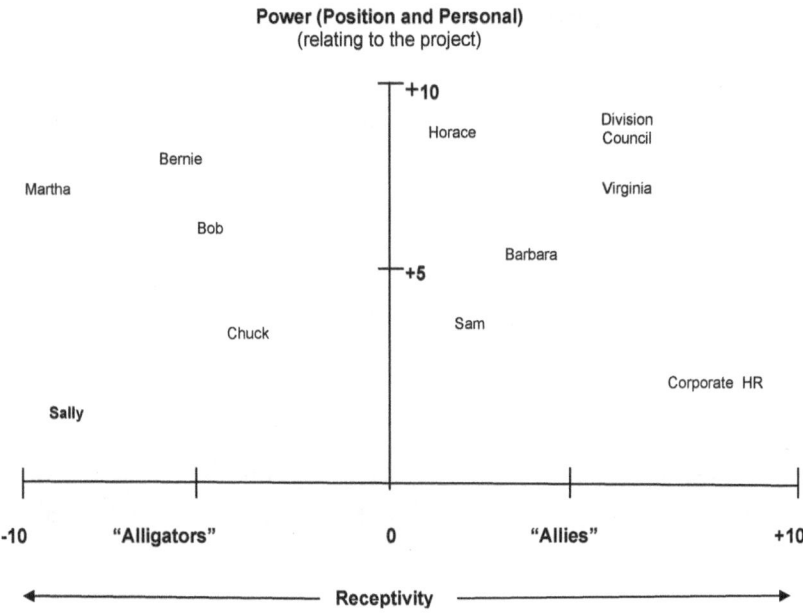

In reaching out to your key stakeholders, remember it is unlikely that they will share the same missionary zeal you have for the project. They may not know much about it. Perhaps they will become more excited and positive once you educate them on the possible benefits to the organization, and to them and their responsibilities. Perhaps not. But regardless of their initial or ongoing reaction, the very fact you reached out to stakeholders and genuinely listened to their thoughts and ideas is bound to have a positive effect. You communicated that you value them and see them as critical to the success of the project.

Determine which mode or modes of communication you are going to use. That is, face-to-face meetings, focus groups, telephone calls, questionnaires, and so forth. Also think about how and when you are going to update them regarding project progress.

Force Field Analysis

The Force Field Analysis tool is an excellent way for you to identify what lies ahead on the journey you are going to take to achieve your project objective. You should be in a good position to apply this tool after you have received your key stakeholders' inputs as discussed above.

Force Field Analysis helps to identify and analyze the forces that may foster or hinder change.

Change occurs when the forces to make something different are greater than the forces to keep it the same. When we want to cause change, we can get valuable information by considering these forces and their intensity. The Force Field is a way to do this, and to make change happen.

This tool is especially valuable to remind you to identify the restraining forces as well as the driving forces for change. Often, in our excitement to initiate a change or action that we are zealous about we neglect to consider restraining forces. In making change, we need to think of ways to lessen resistance as well as to push the benefits or driving forces of the change.

In constructing a Force Field Diagram, the forces encouraging the change, the *driving forces*, are put on the left in the diagram or status quo line. The *restraining forces* are put on the right-hand side of the diagram or status quo line. The length of the arrows used can indicate the strength of the various forces. The longer the line, the greater the strength of the driver or resister.

The insight gained by using this tool can help you think through appropriate strategies and steps to build into your work plan for implementing your objective.

An example of a Force Field Diagram is shown on the following page.

BUILDING BLOCK #2: CLARITY: DEVELOPING SHARED EXPECTATIONS

Figure 4.9 Example: Force Field Analysis

Objective: Refocus our efforts to keep our continuous improvement strategy vibrant and moving forward for the next two years in serving as a positive catalyst for identifying and implementing improvements in our organizational capability.

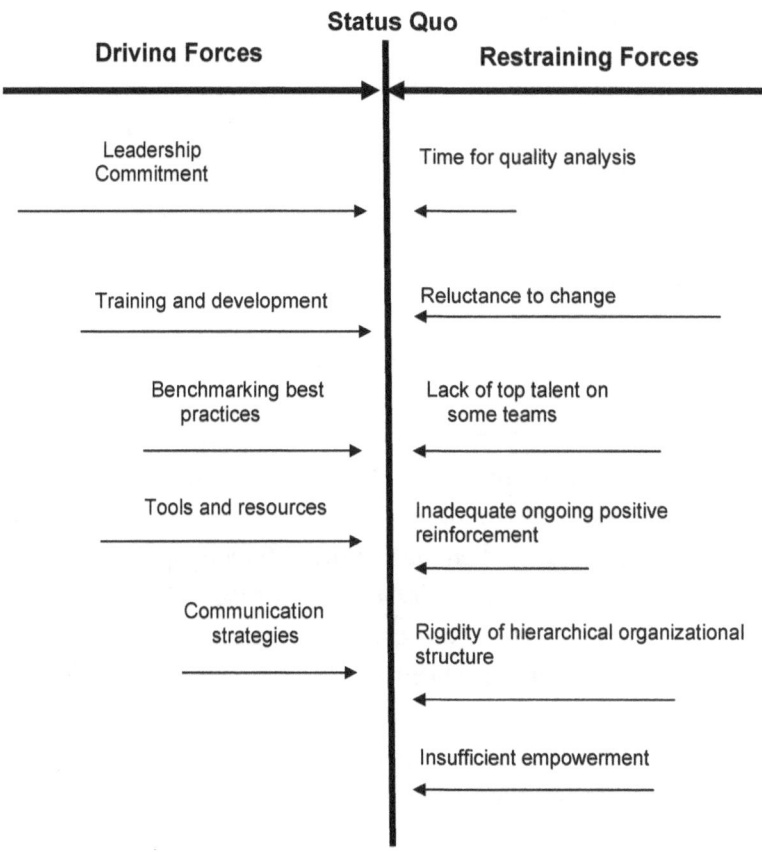

Risk Management

Risk Management is about identifying ahead of time what might go wrong in implementing your project and what preventive or contingent actions you might take to counteract such possibilities.

How to use

Risk Assessment

1. Review your Project Specifications and identify anything that might go wrong, that is, potential problems.
2. Assess the probability and seriousness of such problems occurring.

Risk Planning

Review your Risk Assessment and:

1. Plan any appropriate *preventive actions*. That is, actions designed to prevent such problems from occurring.
2. Develop any appropriate *contingent actions*. That is, actions to take if and when the identified potential problems might surface. As applicable, also identify a "trigger". That is, what will cause you to initiate the contingent action for each potential problem? Identify a person responsible for initiating the appropriate remedial action.
3. As applicable, embed appropriate steps or detail in your work plan to cover identified preventive or contingent actions.

3. Work Breakdown Structure: Scoping Out the Work to Be Done

Where You Are

- You have defined project specifications that are understood and accepted by the key project stakeholders.
- You have identified and analyzed implementation challenges. Some of the results of your analysis will no doubt find their way into the detailing of your work.

Work Breakdown Structure (WBS): A methodology for identifying and grouping the various work packages and related tasks to be included in your work plan. It is the map or outline for your work plan.

The work breakdown structure is a valuable transitional methodology used between generating your project specifications and crafting your work plan. On less complex projects, again getting back to scalability, you may not find a need for a WBS or a work plan.

On the other hand, again with less complex projects, you may find it beneficial to work straight from the WBS foregoing the need to go into further detail with a work plan. The WBS in such instances serves as a checklist.

The number of levels of breakdown and detail should fit the size and complexity of your project. For most projects, three levels of breakdown are sufficient. The three levels are the project objective, the work packages, and the tasks or activities performed for each work package.

BUILDING COMMITMENT

What to Do:

1. Write down your project objective.

2. Apply the Affinity Diagram tool described in the team tools section of Chapter 6, *Teams: Synergy at* Work, to identify the needed work packages.

3. Identify and list under each work package the tasks that need to be performed in that work package. Reapply the Affinity Diagram if needed.

Below is an example of a work breakdown structure.

Figure 4.10 Example: Work Breakdown Structure

Project Objective: Identify and implement strategies to reduce the total costs of general employee training at the operations facility while maintaining the required safety and quality standards and without unduly sacrificing quality of the overall training program.

Work Packages →	Project Formulation	Getting Started	Data Gathering and Analysis	Recommendations
Tasks →	•Develop Project Charter •Get approval	•Select project team •Have initial meeting	•Describe "Future State" •Describe "Current State"	•Develop recommendations •Present recommendations

In this example, the project objective is the first level of breakdown. The work packages are the second level of breakdown. And the bulleted tasks to be performed under each of the work packages are the third level of breakdown.

4. Work Plan: Sequencing and Detailing the Work to Be Done

Where You Are:

- You have articulated project specifications that are understood and accepted by the key project stakeholders.
- You have identified and analyzed implementation challenges. Some of the results of your analysis will no doubt find their way into the detailing of your work plan.
- You have scoped out the work to be done by developing a work breakdown structure.

Work Plan: A methodology for sequencing and detailing the specific work to be done to successfully complete a project.

The work plan format described below works well for most projects. If the complexity of the project warrants it, project management software programs are available, such as Microsoft Project. Such software programs allow for detailed scheduling, resource allocation, and cost planning as well as tracking and reporting progress. There are also additional project planning techniques available such as the Critical Path Method (CPM) and Program Evaluation and Review Technique (PET) for larger, more complex projects. Organizations whose livelihood is project management have staff dedicated to project management.

Work Plan Format

The work plan format is comprised of three components: Program, Schedule, and Resource Allocation. Each of these three components is described below.

Program

Steps	Accountability
The sequence of steps necessary to effectively work the plan. If called for by the rigor of the plan, the steps can be arranged in phases or stages. Also, as needed, important notations regarding the specific step can be summarized under a Detail caption right below the statement of the step.	The person or people accountable for ensuring that a specific step is effectively and efficiently completed.

Schedule

The anticipated *beginning* and *ending* dates *for each step.*

Resource Allocation

An estimate of the resources needed, as applicable, to complete each step.

People	Financial	Space & Equipment	Information
People-days required to complete the specific step.	"Out of pocket" costs, if any, for the specific step.	Special space and equipment needs, if any, to complete the specific step. Often, if there are any special space and equipment needs, the requirement will span several steps, or the project as a whole.	Data or information, if needed, to complete the specific step.

The structure for a complete work plan is shown on the following two pages.

Project Plan

Project Specifications

Business Opportunity or Challenge:

Objective:

Desired Outcomes:

Value:

Key Roles and Authorities:

Timing: Start:
             Completion:

                                                    Date prepared:

BUILDING COMMITMENT

Page 1 of

Work Plan

Program Steps	Acct.	Schedule		Resource Allocation			Information
		Begin	End	People	Financial	Space & Equipment	

Project Control

Just as the complexity of the project should dictate the rigor of the project planning process, the control methods used to monitor and modify work in progress should mirror the magnitude and complexity of the work plan. The work plan format described above has proven to be sufficient for most leaders to monitor progress on projects they are accountable for.

You as the leader will definitely want to have regular progress review checkpoints, perhaps pegged as project milestones. You may want to schedule project progress meetings with the key project players. If it is applicable to a particular project, you may want to specify quantifiable measures to help you monitor progress.

5. BUILDING BLOCK #3: PERFORMANCE COACHING: GUIDING SUCCESS

> The first order of business is to build a group of people who under the influence of the institution, grow taller and become healthier, stronger, and more autonomous.
>
> –Robert K. Greenleaf

Where We Are

The intent of the first building block for building commitment, *Selection*, discussed in chapter 3, was to provide you with a practical and proven process to assure that you arrange for a good fit between the opportunity you have and the individual attributes and passion needed for a person or people to perform in an exemplary way.

The intent of the second building block, *Clarity*, discussed in chapter 4, was to provide you with practical and proven methodologies to develop shared expectations with your associate relative to both ongoing results, that is, role and responsibilities, and time-limited results, that is, goals and actions.

After assuring a good fit and developing shared expectations with your associate you need to develop an effective working relationship centered on the work to be done to capitalize on your investment. You do that through performance coaching.

What Is "Performance Coaching"?

Performance Coaching: Ongoing one-on-one work-centered quality conversations between a supervising manager and associate to provide timely and appropriate direction, guidance, and support to help the associate succeed in achieving desired results.

Performance coaching involves frequent conversations about reinforcing expectations, achieving those expectations, specific work, and the associate's needs. In addition to improving work planning and execution in achieving desired results, such conversations serve to build constructive working relationships. Not by idle chatter or schmoozing, but by genuine work-related authentic exchanges.

It is important to realize that we are not talking about bully bossing or micro-managing here. But rather, having a strong, highly engaged manager who has ongoing work conversations tailored to the individual and the situation.

Performance coaching is tailored to the organizational level of the associate; the nature of the work, and the associate's development or maturity level relative to the position's role and responsibilities, or specific projects, assignments, or tasks.

At the front lines of management such conversations could occur several times a day to discuss current operational matters. At senior levels the manager and associate will most likely have such conversations far less frequently with the focus most times being on strategic rather than operational matters.

The Under-Management Epidemic

Organizations are increasingly realizing the value of performance coaching. It is a top talent management best practice. It reinforces and significantly increases the application and productivity of training efforts. Associates of effective performance coaches outperform associates of managers who do not provide or provide ineffective performance coaching.

Despite the value of performance coaching relative to achieving desired results and associate development, my experience in working with leaders and teams at all organizational levels for years is that there is insufficient performance coaching, both in the amount and quality of such coaching.

In his book, *It's Okay to Be the Boss*[1], Bruce Tulgan argues that there is an under-management epidemic.

He cites several reasons or myths for this epidemic:

- **The Myth of Empowerment:** *The way to empower people is to leave them alone and let them manage themselves.* The truth is that people perform better with more direction, guidance, and support. Letting people do their thing without the proper direction, guidance, and support is "false empowerment", not "real empowerment".

- **The Myth of Fairness:** *The way to be fair is to treat everyone the same.* What is truly fair is doing more for some people and less for others, based on their performance.

- **The Myth of the Nice Guy:** *The only way to be strong is to act like a jerk, but I want to be a "nice guy".* Real "nice guy" managers do what it takes to help employees succeed so those employees can achieve desired results.

- **The Myth of the Difficult Conversation:** *Being hands-off is the way to avoid difficult conversations with employees.* Being a weak manager makes difficult conversations inevitable. Whereas being a strong manager means difficult conversations rarely occur, and when they do happen, they are not so painful after all.

- **The Myth of Red Tape:** *Managers are prevented from being strong because there are so many factors beyond their control–red tape, corporate culture, senior management, limited resources.* Focusing on the many factors that *are* within a manager's control is the way to be a stronger manager. Also, learning the rules and the red tape allows the manager to work within and around them.

- **The Myth of the Natural Leader:** *I am not "good at" managing.* The best managers are people—natural or not—who have a genuine desire to manage, learn practical and proven methods to do so, and, engage in deliberate practice to continually improve their management competence.

- **The Myth of Time:** *There is not enough time to manage people.* Since time is so limited, the manager definitely does not have time to deal with all the things that can go wrong if the proper time is not allocated to spend time upfront managing people.

The Coaching Spectrum

The Coaching Spectrum below outlines the various behaviors that you as a manager can use in providing timely and appropriate guidance and support to each of your associates.

Figure 5.1 The Coaching Spectrum

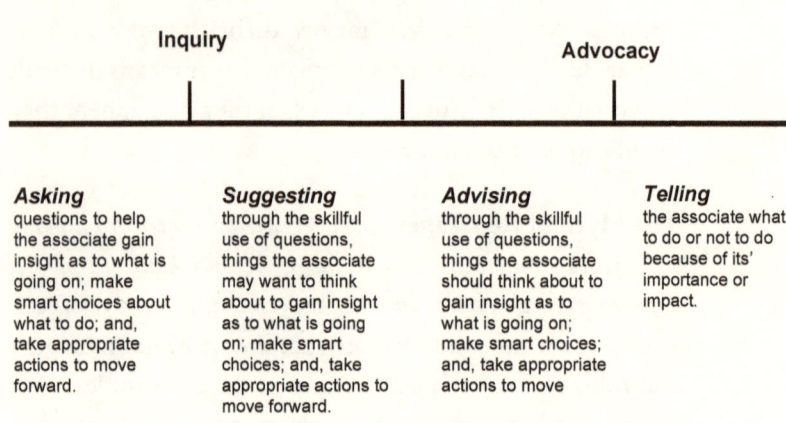

Asking questions to help the associate gain insight as to what is going on; make smart choices about what to do; and, take appropriate actions to move forward.

Suggesting through the skillful use of questions, things the associate may want to think about to gain insight as to what is going on; make smart choices; and, take appropriate actions to move forward.

Advising through the skillful use of questions, things the associate should think about to gain insight as to what is going on; make smart choices; and, take appropriate actions to move

Telling the associate what to do or not to do because of its' importance or impact.

Coaching purists will argue with including telling in the spectrum. I vigorously disagree. Telling, which includes teaching, is certainly appropriate when a person is new to a specific position, project, assignment or task; when safety is involved; or when there are performance discrepancies that need to be addressed.

Approaches to Managing

The key in determining what behaviors to use as a manager in providing performance coaching is to pace with your associate's developmental or maturity level. That is, to pace with your associate's competence and commitment, relative to their specific work responsibilities. You as the manager should be *directive* when interacting with an associate who is immature relating to a particular role, responsibility, project, assignment, or task. *Collaborative* with a more mature associate. And, use a *delegative* approach with a mature associate. But regardless of your associate's general maturity level, you need to adjust your approach when the person is more or less mature given a particular assignment or project.

The continuum below shows the various you as a manager have in managing your associate or work group.

Figure 5.2 Approaches to Managing Continuum

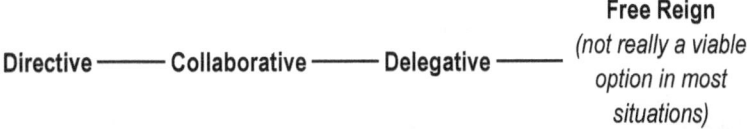

As you move from left to right on the continuum, increasingly more discretion is provided the associate or work group in planning, executing, and controlling the work.

Figure 5.3 Defining the Various Managing Approaches

Directive: Characterized by "telling". That is, what to do, why to do it, when to do it, how to do it, and so forth. A high degree of teaching.

Collaborative: Characterized by discussion and consultation with one another regarding desired results (the WHATS) and the process(es) to be used, the challenges, and decisions to be made (the HOWS).

Delegative: Characterized by agreeing on the WHATS, and allowing ample associate discretion regarding the HOWS.

Regardless of the approach called for, you will always want to look for opportunities to provide encouragement, constructive feedback, and, as earned, appreciation. Taken together with your conversations about the work, the message comes across loud and clear that you care. And the hidden message—really not so hidden—is that you think the individual is important.

The chart below illustrates what has been discussed relative to pacing with your associate's maturity level when providing performance coaching.

Figure 5.4 Matching Managing Approach and Associate Maturity Level

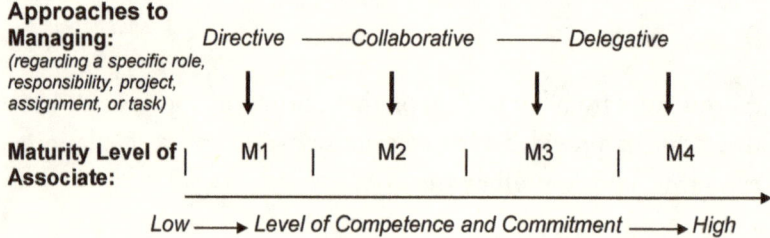

Some Important Points

- As an associate matures, work through the managerial approaches in order and slowly. For example, do not skip from Directive to Delegative.

- Do not make the mistake of taking your high performers for granted.

- Realize that people will develop at different rates and to different levels. If an associate does not have the ability to fully mature into being a high performer, you should view that as being okay as long you did not select the associate expressly for their high potential, and the associate is committed and performing at a satisfactory level. It is unlikely, and perhaps unrealistic, to think that everyone, despite your hopes and managerial acumen, will be a high performer.

- If a mature associate regresses, you can move quickly to a strong intervention and directive approach if and when needed since the person has already been through the previous developmental stage or stages.

- Your ultimate performance coaching goal is to enable your associates to self-correct and continuously improve without a lot of direction and guidance. Of course, you want to and need to continue to provide encouragement.

Diagnosis and Range

Your capability to determine the most appropriate managing approach called for *(Diagnosis)* is obviously important. But you also need to have the behavioral flexibility to be able to use the approach called for *(Range)*.

Figure 5.4 Range and Diagnosis

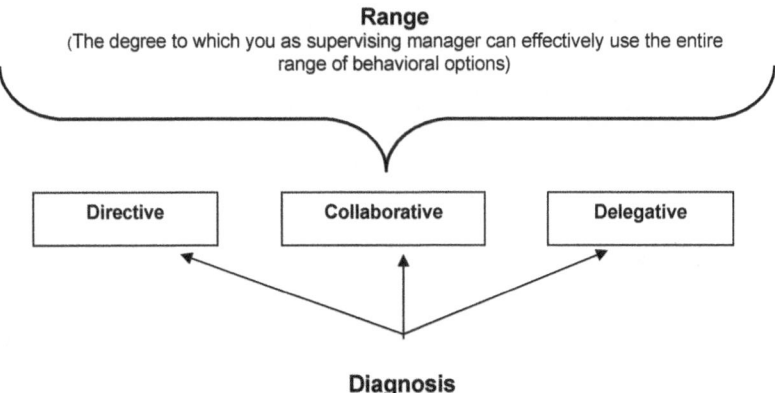

Self-Assessment

- What is your current skill level in being able to diagnose your associates' maturity level relative to current responsibilities, projects, assignments, or tasks?

- What is your current skill and comfort level in being able to move up and down the approaches in the managing continuum, changing your managing approach to fit your associates' current maturity relative to their respective roles and responsibilities, projects, assignments, and maturity?

Based on your assessment, what specific development needs do you have in either accurately diagnosing situations or being able to effectively use the entire range of managing approaches? What would be an appropriate development plan for you to improve in these areas?

Making Performance Coaching Happen

Unearthing Everyday Opportunities

Once you understand the importance of performance coaching and the positive results that can be achieved from it, you will not have a difficult time finding opportunities and occasions to appropriately interact with your associates.

Large challenges your associates are wrestling with can readily be identified as coaching opportunities. Smaller opportunities are not as easy to spot. Such things as writing a specific report; approaching a colleague on a sticky matter; or how to respond to a customer inquiry.

These smaller or more subtle coaching opportunities are discovered by getting out of your office and adopting the practice of *Caring*

BUILDING BLOCK #3: PERFORMANCE COACHING: GUIDING SUCCESS

by Walking Around (CBWA)[2]. CBWA provides you with valuable personal observation input as to how things are going. But it also provides you with valuable "in the moment" coaching opportunities. The key is that you need to be genuine, truly care, and listen attentively. You are not out there to snoop around. Think of it as "cultivating serendipity."

Working on Larger Ticket Items

You will want to be on the alert to carve out time to engage in quality thinking and interacting with your associates on the larger, more visible opportunities and challenges they may face. Such things as planning a big project; solving a vexing problem; or making an important decision.

One-on-One Meetings

Scheduling quality time with each of your key reports on an ongoing basis is a highly recommended practice with huge upside potential. Yet many managers fail to make use of this effective practice. We are talking about nurturing the practice of setting time aside on an ongoing basis to do some quality thinking and interacting around both strategic and operational opportunities and challenges, as well as the associate's personal and professional development.

Managers who claim they do not have the luxury of time to adopt such a practice need to ask themselves what better investment of time they can think of than interacting with their key players on a quality, ongoing basis to assure individual and team success.

The guidelines below have proven useful to managers and their key reports in having one-on-one meetings on an ongoing basis.

Scheduling and Time

- Agree on a schedule that fits your needs. A common practice is to set aside perhaps a maximum of an hour or two every few weeks to get together. Do not use the whole time if you do not need to.

- Within the basic agreement as to the general frequency of meetings, think about scheduling specific meetings on a "rolling calendar" basis rather than having set days and times scheduled far in advance. Scheduling on a rolling calendar allows for needed flexibility for personal commitments and to pace with what is going on operationally, time away or time off, and the like. Sometimes you may want to meet more frequently; other times you may want to extend the time between meetings.

- For new relationships, meet more frequently at the outset of the relationship.

- Treat such meetings as a priority and commit to the scheduled meeting.

Location

- Assuming you can meet in person, consider meeting in your associate's office or work location.

- Geographical proximity will obviously influence the frequency as well as the mode of meetings. When distance is an issue, you will need to consider possible viable alternatives such as telephone, teleconferencing, or making visits to one another.

Agenda

- These meetings need to be viewed as an opportunity to have quality two-way conversations relative to what is going on. Such meetings provide ample opportunities for you as the manager to provide performance coaching.

- Strive to have these meetings be owned more by your associate than yourself as the manager.

- Do not jeopardize the value of engaging in meaningful ongoing dialogue in such meetings by using them as a vehicle for assigning work. There of course, based on operating considerations and efficiencies, need to be exceptions,

- Do not over-structure such meetings. Agree on the agenda at the outset of the meeting.

- Set aside the first part of the meeting to discuss operating matters that the both of you have saved up for each other. This is a wonderful time management practice. Set up a file for each other to toss in notes relative to items to be discussed in your next one-on-one meeting. Obviously, if something cannot wait, go ahead and discuss and do not wait for the one-on-one meeting.

  Devote the second part of the meeting to discuss any pertinent strategic opportunities or challenges, and personal development. If appropriate, reserve a periodic one-on-one meeting just to discuss strategic matters rather than running the risk of having them not get the attention they deserve.

- Periodically discuss the relationship.

Assuming a satisfactory working relationship exists, asking each other the following questions periodically allows for constructive feedback, the opportunity to calibrate the relationship to each other's current needs, and to make the resultant and appropriate behavioral adjustments.

The questions:

- *"What would you like me to **do more of**, or **start doing**?"*
- *"What would you like me to **do less of**, or **stop doing**?"*

In responding to these questions, you as manager do not necessarily have to agree with the constructive feedback. But treat the input as a gift and use it as a basis for an effective dialogue as to what changes you are willing to make or not willing to make, and why.

Periodically using this practice to calibrate your relationship with each of your associates requires a certain amount of vulnerability. Vulnerability is being open about challenges facing you. You should not see it as a weakness and be threatened by it.

Being vulnerable means having the courage to be sincere, open, and honest. It also means being receptive to the input of others. A balance of truthfulness and sensitivity creates a healthy environment in which people can learn and grow.

A Useful Coaching Model

The *GROW* Model[3] is a useful framework to guide coaching conversations, be they simple or complex. The acronym, GROW, affords not only an easy way to remember the steps in the process, but also serves as a reminder of the intent of performance coaching, that is, to help your associates succeed, and learn and grow in so doing.

The GROW Model provides a logical progression in helping you as coach guide an associate in working through an issue. The sample questions shown on the following page are the types of inquiries that are useful in keeping the coaching conversation on track and getting to the crux of each phase of the model. It is not intended that all the questions be asked, or asked as phrased. Again, these are just sample questions. You as the coach may have other types of questions that you may want to ask to bring out useful information or to get the associate to think about a particular aspect of the issue being worked on. Many times, your associate will answer many of the questions without a probe by you as the coach.

Figure 5.5 The Grow Model

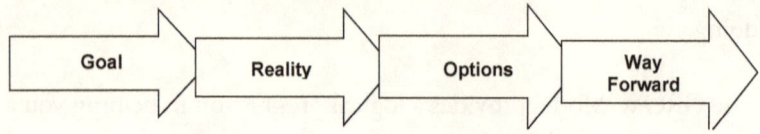

Potential Questions

Goal
What is the goal?
- What are you/we trying to achieve?
- What are the desired outcomes?
- Why is it important?
- How committed are you?

Reality
What is the current situation?
- What is going on now?
- What have you tried? How has it worked?
- What obstacles exist?
- What kind of support do you need/have?

Options
What's possible?
- What are the realistic alternatives?
- What is the best alternative or combination of alternatives? Why?
- What will it take to succeed?
- What are the implementation challenges?

Way **F**orward
What's the best way to proceed?
- What specifically are you going to do?
- What are you willing to commit to?
- What are the steps and timing?
- How are you going to measure progress?
- What help might you need?

The Art of Delegating

The art of delegating is a critical skill in performing your role as a leader-manager and gaining commitment from your associates. Below are some concepts relative to delegating that will serve you well.

Delegation: To entrust responsibility and authority to others and create accountability for results.

Delegating involves passing on to others either ongoing or time-limited responsibilities. That is, you can delegate a piece of work that you have been performing on an ongoing basis as part of your organizational role; or, a project, a portion of a project, or specific task that has a beginning and an end.

Delegation is not:

- Passing the buck.
- Giving up your overall accountability.
- Refusing to make a decision by assigning it to another.
- Shirking personal responsibility.

> **For delegation to be truly effective, it needs to be looked upon as an investment rather than a way of getting rid of work. It needs to be results-driven versus activity-driven.**

Delegation Checklist

The checklist below provides useful guidelines for thinking through and interacting when making an important delegation. The list is comprehensive. The importance, complexity, and length of the assignment you are delegating and the task-relevant competence of the person or people to whom you are delegating will govern the appropriate thoroughness you will use in applying these guidelines to your specific situation.

Remember that delegation is not just pushing work on. It is an excellent opportunity to provide performance coaching and to develop people as well as assign work. Trust and open communications are vital.

When there is a lack of trust on either side, or poor communication, the needed understanding and commitment is unlikely to be there.

There are two component parts to delegating–intent and execution.

Intent

A quality conversation needs to take place when making an important delegation to assure understanding regarding:

The Situation (The Context)

- What is going on?
- Why this assignment?
- Why you?
- Why now?
- What are the given factors (the givens)?
  - Scope and boundaries?
  - Commitments and limitations, e.g., resources, time, and so forth?
- Who are the key stakeholders and players?

The Whats (The Results)

- What's the objective?
- What are the desired outcomes? (How do we know success when we see it?)
- What are our concerns? (What do we need to keep an eye on?)

Execution

A quality conversation needs to take place when making an important delegation to assure understanding regarding the considerations listed and discussed below.

Level of Authority

The chart below can guide your thinking relative to the appropriate amount of authority to delegate relative to a specific project, assignment, or task.

Figure 5.6 Level of Authority

Level of Authority	*Description*
Investigate	Look into the situation. Gather the data and report back to me. I'll decide what to do.
Recommend	Look into the situation and give me your thoughts on what to do. I'll then decide what to do.
Decide and Get Approval	Examine the issue and decide what you are going to do; but don't take action until you check with me first and get my approval.
Act and Inform	Decide what you think needs to be done; do it; and let me know how it turned out.
Act	Take action. No further contact with me is necessary.

Assistance Needed

- Any special training or help needed?
- Any advance communications with others needed regarding the delegation?
    - Who needs to know?
    - What do we need to tell them?
    - How are we going to tell them?

Working Together

- How are we going to work together regarding this delegation?
- What is the frequency and kind of interaction needed?

The frequency, type, and amount of interaction should be governed by the length and complexity of the project, assignment, or task being delegated, the relevant maturity of the person receiving the delegation, and the level of authority granted.

The Hows (Performing)

The action plan.
- What?
- Who?
- When?
- Resources needed?

Moving from the WHATS to the HOWS

A good practice is for you as the supervising manager, after assuring that the WHATS are understood, is to leave it up to the person or people to whom the responsibility is being delegated to figure out and implement the HOWS, assuming that their relevant maturity warrants.

But life is never that simple. The line between the WHATS and HOWS needs to be a dotted line, not a solid line.

On important projects or assignments you may have some definite ideas on how the work should be done, You need to communicate your thoughts or desires. You should however welcome and arrange for meaningful input on the WHATS from those going to be doing the work, especially if they possess relevant knowledge and expertise.

Other times, for various reasons, it may be appropriate for you as the manager to be actively engaged in the HOWS. That is, planning and executing the work, including monitoring and modifying work in progress. This is especially true if the person or people to whom the delegation is being made are short on relevant knowledge and experience.

The important thing is that when delegating important responsibilities there needs to be a quality conversation on the front end to reach a common understanding as to the intent of the assignment, and the role, responsibilities, and authorities of the respective parties in its execution.

Monitoring Assignments

There is an old management adage: *"What the boss inspects, the boss expects"*. Translated, this means that if you as the manager delegate something and no longer pay attention to it, you are sending a message that it cannot be all that important and you do not care all that much.

Use the practice described below to monitor the projects, assignments, or tasks you delegate.[4]

Think of your delegations as *gremlins*.

There are three key principles to follow in managing gremlins.

1. Keep a gremlin *inventory*.

    The gremlin inventory need not be sophisticated. Maintain a simple listing for each of your direct reports. List the dates and nature of each of the delegated assignments. Have a column to make progress notes. Keep the list in a manila folder you keep for each of your immediate reports. You can also use this folder to keep notes regarding performance and items to be discussed in your next one-on-one meeting.

2. Feed or shoot the gremlins—don't let them starve to death.

Regularly feed the gremlins. That is, talk to your associate or associates about how the assignment is going. On larger projects, the feeding schedule might be determined by project milestone dates. Your one-on-one meetings are a good time for feeding.

You and your immediate reports may have to adjust the respective gremlin inventories periodically in light of current realities. The priorities placed on the various gremlins may change, or workload balance concerns may arise. Some gremlins may just have to be shot. Others postponed. But whatever you do, do not let them starve to death. You need to feed and nurture them on a regular basis, or shoot them.

3. Keep the gremlins in their right cages.

In an effort to help or rescue your immediate reports, you, from time to time may inadvertently take back some gremlins (upward delegation). But try not to do so. You, of course, should help your people, but just remember who owns the gremlin. And see to it that it remains in its proper cage.

Capturing Learning

You should call periodic "time outs" with your team and direct reports to assess *both* results and process. Such time outs could occur at the end of an important project or major assignment; in one-on-one meetings; or just at certain times just to take the pulse.

Taking the time to capture and apply learning has big time payouts, especially considering the brief time it takes to do so.

Listed below are some questions you may want to use.

For a post-project debrief:

- "What did we set out to do?"
- "What actually happened?"
- "Why did it happen?"
- "What have we learned?"
- "What, if anything, are we going to do next time?"

For general results:

- "How are things going?"
- "What is working well?"
- "What needs improving?", and, if needed, "How are we going to improve?"
- "What specific opportunities or challenges are presenting themselves?"

For a process assessment:

- "How is the process working?"
- "What, if anything thing needs to be modified?", and, if needed, what changes need to be made?"
- "How are we going to implement the changes?"

Constructive Feedback and Encouragement

Research continually tells us that a high priority people at work have is to know how they are doing. Most likely you do not have your associates asking you this question. But you can rest assured that they want to know. Being an effective performance coach and using the concepts and practices in this book will go a long way in letting your associates know just how they are doing.

In addition to you as the supervising manager there are many sources of potential feedback for people as to just how they are doing at work.

Figure 5.7 Sources of Feedback

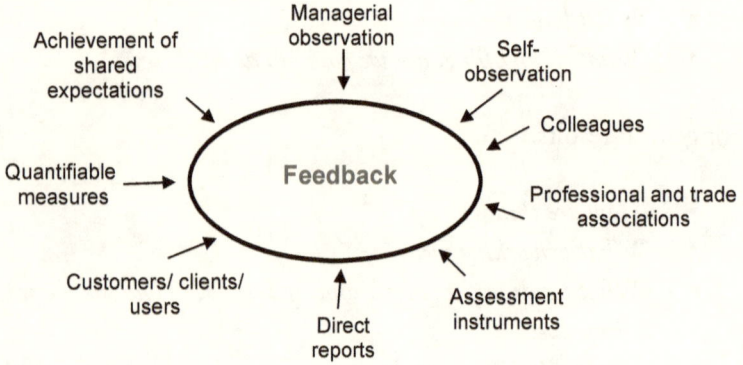

Constructive Feedback

Constructive feedback is based on observation and interpretation of specific behaviors, be they positive, negative, or neutral.

Praise and *criticism* on the other hand, is feedback based on judgments and generalizations and conclusions regarding the person himself or herself. The difference between constructive feedback and praise and criticism is an important distinction.

Rather than express one's opinion about the person, constructive feedback provides specific information and fosters communication regarding specific behaviors that the one providing the feedback would like to see continued (positive reinforcement); or, improved or discontinued (negative reinforcement).

To be effective, constructive feedback needs to be earned, timely specific, personalized, and genuine.

> Catch people doing things right and let them know about it, in no uncertain terms.
>
> –Bob Mager

Encouragement

Encouragement is a powerful form of feedback. It is positive information that tells one that she on the right track, making progress, and can do it. It is more personal than other forms of feedback. Encouragement requires you to get close to people and show them you care.

Continuous Learning and Growth

A primary focus and benefit of your performance coaching is to help your associates to continuously learn and grow. To enhance their role-related maturity level. Part of this development comes from education and training. But the environment that you set in encouraging people to learn and grow and guiding them in doing so through your performance coaching is the key ingredient to continuous learning and growth. And, reinforcing training through your performance coaching makes for an unbeatable combination.

And remember, that in developing people your role is not to fix them, but to help them realize their potential. People really do not change that much. Sure, you want to help your associates to perhaps make some minor behavioral adjustments that may help them improve in their current roles. But do not try and overhaul them. People can always improve, but you need to work with what is there.

You need to be diligent about keeping individual performance expectations a little bit larger than each of your associates to allow for challenge, growth, and increasing contributions.

Figure 5.8 Evolving Performance Expectations

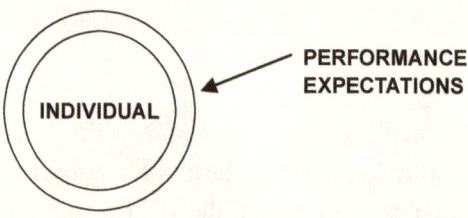

You can think of times when the challenge you faced was slightly greater than your role-related maturity level. You typically do your best work in these situations. In such situations, you are "in the flow". You are performing effortlessly and skillfully despite the difficulty of the experience. The challenge is a stretch, but you are confident that you are up to the challenge.

Michael Csikszentmihalyl has specialized in studying the relationship of challenge and competence to optimal performance.[5] The chart shown below helps to understand this important concept of the relationship of challenge and competence and attempting to evolve performance expectations to be slightly larger than the individual as he matures.

Figure 5.9 Optimal Performance: Matching Challenge and Competence

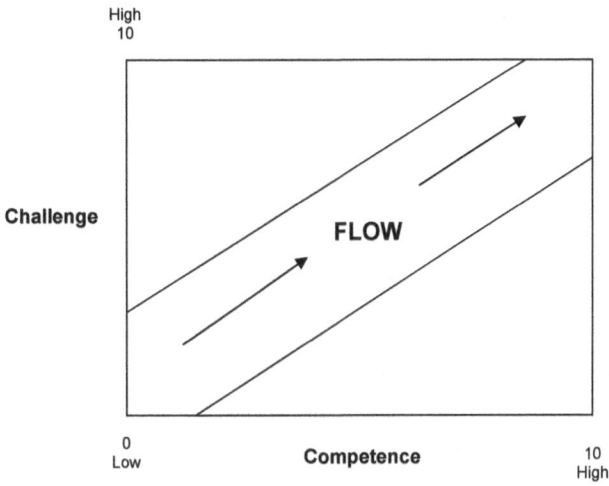

Increasing Challenge in One's Current Position

There are two ways to increase challenge in a person's current position–*content* and *discretion*.

Content

> The position content is reengineered by expanding the scope of the ongoing responsibilities assigned to a person and thus allowing for a more "meaningful whole." The person, for example, is allowed to handle more tasks in a specific work flow or value chain, creating greater challenge and motivational power. In his pioneering work on motivation, Frederick Herzberg termed this important concept "job enrichment"[6]. He admonished that job enrichment should not be confused with job enlargement, which is giving a person greater amount of the same work. Herzberg goes on to emphasize that giving a person more of the same is not job enrichment; that is job enlargement.

Discretion

Greater discretion entails giving a person more latitude or authority to plan and control his work. Examples of this important principle are to assign a person the responsibility for a specific internal or external client or customer group, a geographical area, or a specific product or service.

Increasing Challenge Outside of One's Current Position

Ways to afford additional challenge and developmental opportunities beyond one's current position include such things as project assignments, temporary rotational or relief assignments, or being a member of an ad hoc team such as a process improvement or product launch team.

Managing Performance Discrepancies

A performance discrepancy is the difference between what you want to have happening, the SHOULDs, and what is happening, the ACTUALs.

Experiencing performance discrepancies is inevitable. For example, someone new to your group will most likely lack the maturity level to perform the complete responsibilities of the new position. Hopefully, time, experience, and your performance coaching will resolve this performance discrepancy.

Most times you as a manager are able to analyze and resolve performance discrepancies based on your intuitive intelligence. That is, having a good sense of what is going on and what is needed based upon your wisdom. Wisdom being your practical know-how based on experience.

But as important as intuition is, it is sometimes insufficient or unreliable. It may be the problem is complicated or uncertain; you lack the needed relevant expertise to solve it; your inputs are incomplete or distorted; you need to involve others in the solution; or, perhaps you need to look at the problem in a different way.

This is where *deliberate analysis* comes in. On such occasions, you need to see and use intuitive intelligence and deliberate analysis as complementary to each other rather than as separate approaches to problem solving and decision-making. This synthesis is most effective when you use analysis to support your intuitive intelligence.

Figure 5.10 Synthesis of Intuitive Intelligence and Deliberate Analysis

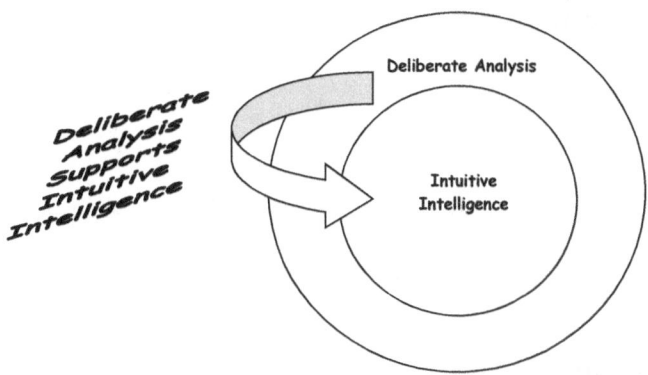

There are several benefits of using a proven decision-making process. They include:

- As discussed above, deliberate analysis complements and balances your intuitive intelligence.

    - This synthesis helps you to use your rational mode of thinking (left brain) in conjunction with your spontaneous mode of thinking (right brain).

- It also allows for deeper and more comprehensive thinking when your instinctive or "gut feeling" is not enough.

- Provides for an orderly thought process.

    The flow in a sound decision-making model allows you to address the problem or decision in a logical, sequential manner rather than "butterflying around."

- Optimizes group work.

    A sound, shared process allows you to channel the various personalities, divergent knowledge, skills, experience, and viewpoints of people working on the challenge to make for more efficient and effective results.

Performance Analysis

Performance Analysis is deliberate analysis applied to people concerns.

Performance Analysis:	A process for identifying the nature, cause, and appropriate resolution of a performance discrepancy. A performance discrepancy is the difference between what should be happening and what is actually happening. In other words, a performance gap.

The intent here is to provide you with a comprehensive, rational, repeatable process that fosters quality thinking and interacting in analyzing and resolving performance problems. The process has been successfully taught to and used by managers and their advisors in all types of organizational settings. This practical and proven process will provide you with greater clarity, confidence, and competence in addressing performance concerns or problems that are worth doing something about, and when the resolution is not obvious.[7]

In presenting this process I want to first have you take a look at the model on the next page. The model presents a good bird's eye view of the various factors impacting individual performance at work. Then, making use of the model as a good backdrop, we will go through the flow of the performance analysis model.

Figure 5.11 Factors Affecting Performance at Work[8]

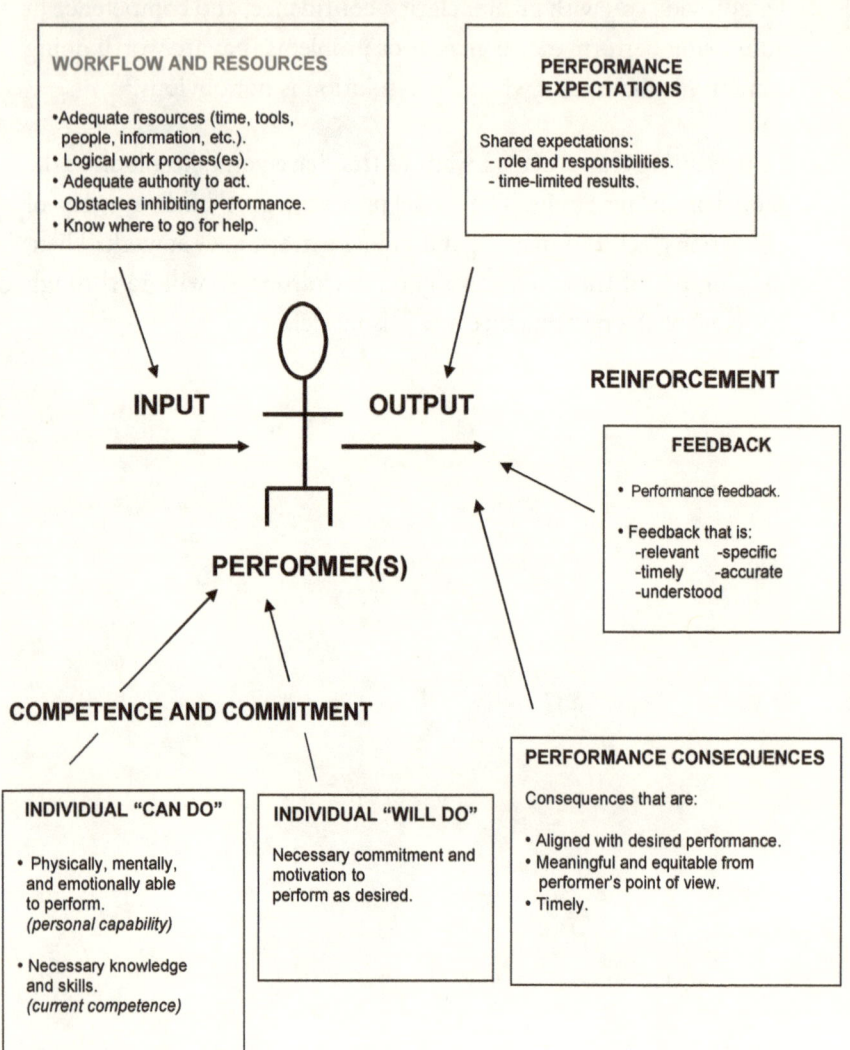

Now let us take a look at the performance analysis process flow. The flow is presented in the context of a sound decision-making framework that can be used for all kinds of problem solving and decision-making, not just resolving performance discrepancies.[9]

Figure 5.12 Five-Stage Decision-Making Framework

1. **Framing** — Determining from what viewpoint the decision will be made.

2. **Gathering Intelligence** — Gathering relevant data and inputs from appropriate sources.

3. **Coming to Conclusions** — Making an efficient and effective decision using a systematic approach based on sound framing and good intelligence.

4. **Implementing** — Crafting an appropriate course of action.

5. **Learning from Experience** — Capturing both outcomes and process learning to improve efficiency and effectiveness in the future.

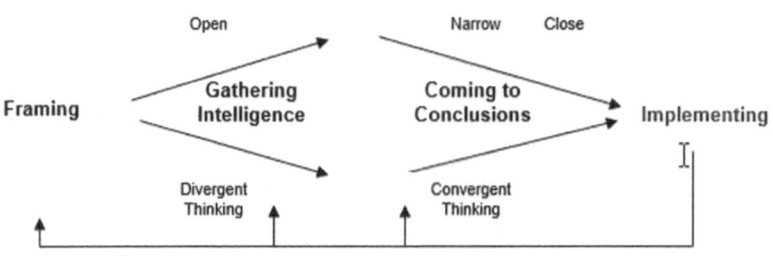

The Performance Analysis Process

Stage 1: Framing

> If I had an hour to solve a problem, I'd spend 55 minutes thinking about the problem, and five minutes thinking about the solution.
>
> –Albert Einstein

Framing is a critical step. It sets the stage for the balance of the problem-solving process. We frame art to draw attention to the painting or picture. Framing decisions is no different. The framing step determines from what viewpoint or lens the decision will be made. How the problem is framed influences the thinking and interacting that follows in attempting to analyze and resolve the performance concern.

Guidelines

- State the problem in the form of a positively worded question. For example, "How can I help …?

    The "How can…?" leads to stating the problem in a specific, actionable form. Stating the problem in positive terms tends to open up thinking that gets limited when the problem is framed in negative terms.

- If there are several concerns, separate the problems, at least for the purpose of analysis. In not doing so, you may be trying to deal with a generalized mess.

    If it turns out that there is a common root cause, you can link the problems back up later in resolving the problem. If not, you will customize your resolutions to fit what is going on in each of the performance discrepancies.

BUILDING BLOCK #3: PERFORMANCE COACHING: GUIDING SUCCESS

- Be specific. Avoid generalizations or "fuzzies."

  Use specific behavioral terms rather than abstract fuzzy language. For example, rather than framing the problem in such abstract terms such as "poor planning" or "inadequate quality communications", move to a lower level of abstraction by asking: "How do you know (insert the generalization) when you see it?" The answer to this question will allow you to develop the right level of specificity to get a handle on the problem. The structure provided in the next step of the process, Gathering Intelligence, will help you continue to specify and define the problem. You may even find yourself going back and altering your framing of the problem.

- Do not include possible causes of the performance discrepancy when framing the problem.

  An example of possible premature inclusion of causation in framing the problem would be "How to have Bob be more motivated to…"? Lack of motivation is a possible cause; not a performance discrepancy. If you are sure that Bob lacks the necessary motivation to do whatever, fine. But you may be jumping to conclusions. Let the performance analysis logic do the work for you.

The Process

Using the guidelines above, do the following:

- *Summarize the performance discrepancy in a sentence.*

  Answer: "How can I/we…"

- *Describe the importance of the performance discrepancy by answering the following questions:*

Answer:

"Why is this performance discrepancy important?"
"What would happen if it were left alone?"

Stage 2. Gathering Intelligence

Gathering intelligence involves logically and specifically defining the performance discrepancy. It involves taking a close look at what relevant information you have, what additional information you may need to gather, and what assumptions you may be making. A good problem specification puts you in a position to constructively move ahead and determine the possible causes or causes of the discrepancy. The process described below is a practical and proven method for effectively and efficiently defining the relevant problem specifications.

What to Do

1. **Specify the problem characteristics. "What IS the problem?"**[10]

    Answer the questions below as they relate to the performance discrepancy. *Be precise and continue to pursue each question until you cannot break it done any further.* That is, you want to "Question to a void." Not "avoid", but "a void".

BUILDING BLOCK #3: PERFORMANCE COACHING: GUIDING SUCCESS

WHAT?	(Identification)	What specifically is the discrepancy?
		What more can be said that is not included in the performance discrepancy you crafted in the Framing stage above?
WHO?	(Individual/group)	Who is the person or group with whom you are experiencing the discrepancy?
WHERE?	(Physical or geographical location)	Where is the discrepancy seen?
WHEN?	(Occasion)	Is it a "day one" problem? Or did it occur over time?
		If it is not a "day one" problem", when did the discrepancy first occur?
		When does the discrepancy occur (specific times, tasks, activities, and so forth)?
EXTENT?	(Magnitude/ progression)	How often does the discrepancy occur (number of times, % of the time, and so forth)?
		Is the discrepancy becoming greater, less, or staying the same?

2. **Bracket the problem characteristics by specifying "What IS NOT the problem that could be?"**

Defining the limits of the problem allows you to contrast where the problem occurs and does not occur. Doing so allows you to identity patterns and possibly discover clues to cause. See Figure 5.12 on page 149 below.

In defining the problem, make the IS and IS NOT data as close as possible. That is, describe where the problem is not occurring although it would be reasonable to expect that it might occur there. A "tight" problem specification increases your chances of unveiling key patterns and clues to cause. You want to contrast apples to apples, and not apples to papayas.

In defining the problem, it is more effective to specify the IS and IS NOT data for a particular problem characteristic at the same time rather than to go back to the IS NOT data after specifying the IS data. Doing so will sharpen your analysis.

Before moving on, identify any additional intelligence you need to gather and any assumptions you are making that need to be checked out.

3. **Contrast the IS and IS NOT data to identify patterns and possible clues to cause.**

   Review your IS and IS NOT specifications for each of the problem characteristics and make note of any patterns or possible clues to cause. The question you want to ask is: *"What, if anything, is unique, odd, or different about the IS and IS NOT data as it relates to the performance discrepancy"?*

   The structure below serves as an effective worksheet for you to think through and record your analysis for all three steps described above. As needed, replicate on a sheet of paper and use it to guide your analysis.

Figure 5.12 Gathering Intelligence Framework

	IS (the problem?)	IS NOT (the problem that could be?)	CONTRASTS (what, if anything, is unique, odd, or different about the IS and IS NOT data?)
WHAT?			
WHO?			
WHERE?			
WHEN?			
EXTENT?			

Stage 3. Coming to Conclusions

Having defined or specified the problem to your satisfaction by using the three-step process described in the *Gathering Intelligence* stage of the performance analysis logic, you are now in a position to focus in on causation and resultant resolutions. You do so by using the IS and IS NOT data, and the CONTRASTS information you have identified in your problem specification to explore the various

BUILDING COMMITMENT

factors affecting human performance in searching for possible causes of the discrepancy.

The chart below is designed to guide you through the possible cause or causes of a performance discrepancy. The chart is divided into two potential zones of cause; the *Competence* zone and the *Environmental/ Motivational* zone. Each zone contains specific questions relating to the factors in each zone to help you identify the root causation and an appropriate resultant resolution.

It is important to realize that often the cause of a performance discrepancy may be multi-dimensional, and sometimes may contain contributing causes in both the competence zone and the environmental/ motivational zones.

The chart below provides a logical way to work through the various factors affecting performance as displayed earlier in Figure 5.11 on page 142, *Factors Affecting Performance at Work*.

Figure 5.13 Cause Identification Exploration Paths

CAUSE IDENTIFICATION   **RESOLUTION**

Competency Zone

Knowledge/skill deficiency? → Yes/? → Ability deficiency? → No/? → Arrange training, practice, and/or coaching

Yes →
- Provide job aids
- Reengineer job
- Transfer, demote or terminate
- Optimize current situation

Important Considerations

- The difference between a skill deficiency and an ability deficiency is a critical distinction.

The questions to ask are:

- Could the individuals(s) perform as desired if he/she/they really had to?
- Are the individual(s) knowledge/skills adequate to perform as desired?

If the answers to the above questions are *"yes"*, the cause of the performance discrepancy is *not due to a knowledge/skill deficiency*. What you need to do is investigate possible causation is the environmental/motivational zone shown below.

If the answers to the questions above are *"no"*, a knowledge/skill deficiency exists.

Your question now is:

Could the individual(s) learn to perform as desired given reasonable time and resources for the proper training, practice, and coaching?

If your answer to the above question is *"yes"*, appropriate training, practice, and coaching is called for.

If your answer to the above question is *"no"*, an ability deficiency exists and you need to weigh the appropriate alternatives. That is, provide job aids; reengineer job; transfer, demote, or terminate; or optimize the current situation.

- Distinguishing between a knowledge/skill deficiency and an ability deficiency is not always that easy. When in doubt, treat it as a knowledge/skill deficiency. If it turns out that your reasonable support to help the individual has not produced the desired results, you then should proceed as if an ability deficiency exists.

- A useful analogy in helping to understand the difference between a knowledge/skill deficiency and an ability deficiency is to envision a container and the current liquid level in the container. The container represents one's natural ability of talent in a particular field or area. We all have many containers. Some are large. Some are not. And some we may not even know about. We call these latent abilities.

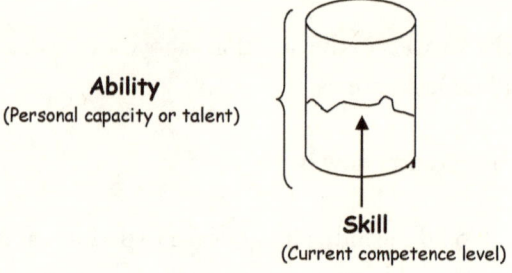

Ability
(Personal capacity or talent)

Skill
(Current competence level)

A person's competence will grow or diminish depending on how much their relevant knowledge and skills are currently honed to perform. A person's ultimate capacity or potential will limit the amount of competence that can be developed in a particular field or endeavor.

And, of course, one's container, or ability, can also grow or shrink over time. This is obvious as we think of the growth in physical and mental capacity of the infant to youth to adult progression. The individual grows both physically and mentally. And, later on, as the individual ages, the physical and mental capability will most likely shrink. One can no longer run, throw, or jump as well as one once did.

And, unfortunately, one's mental acuity will also most likely eventually shrink. Such is life.

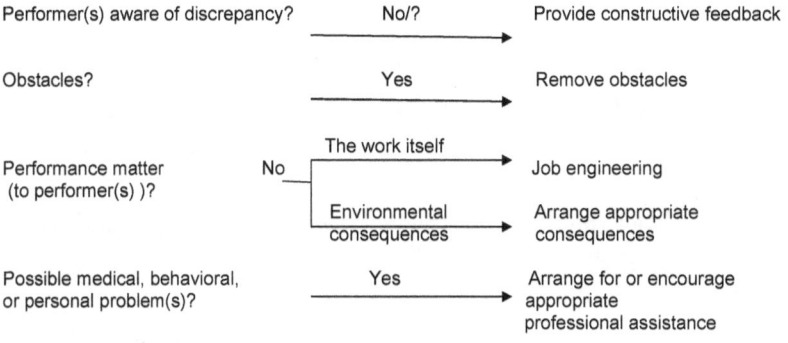

Important Considerations

Performer(s) aware of discrepancy?

The question to ask here is to determine if the performer(s) understands the performance discrepancy that is a concern is to ask yourself if the performer(s) could describe the performance discrepancy, its importance, and dimensions as you have done. If not, a constructive conversation to clarify expectations is in order.

Obstacles?

Questions to ask to uncover possible obstacles:

- Are there any *physical or operational obstacles*, such as work process(es); work layout; lighting; and so forth, that may be getting in the way of the desired performance?

- Are there any *managerial obstacles*, such as unclear or conflicting instructions; enough authority; enough time; and so forth, that may be getting in the way of desired performance?

- Is *performance punishing to the performer*? That is, would the performer's world be a little dimmer by performing as desired?

- Are there *adequate resources*, such as information, equipment, tools, and so forth, for the performer to perform as desired?

- Does the performer know *where to go for help* if and when needed?

If the answer to any or all of the first three questions is *"yes"*, or if the answer to either or both of the last two questions is *"no"*, you may need to work on removing the specific obstacles the question addresses.

Performance matter to the performer(s)?

<u>The work itself</u>

- Does the performer *perceive the work as being meaningful*?

- Is the performer allowed *to exercise an appropriate amount of discretion* in planning, doing, and controlling the work or task in question?

If the answer to either or both of these two questions is *"no"*, you may want to consider possibly enhancing the responsibilities and or discretion afforded to make for a more meaningful challenge.

Consequences surrounding the performance

- Are there *positive consequences* to perform as desired?

- Are there *negative consequences* for not performing as desired?

If the answer to either of these questions is *"no"*, arranging appropriate consequences may be called for.

Is non-performance rewarding?

- Does the individual *get more attention or satisfaction for not performing than performing*?

- By not performing as desired, is the individual *called on less or given less to do*?

If the answer to either of these two questions is *"yes"*, you may need to make some adjustments so that non-performance is not perceived as being rewarding.

Possible medical, behavioral, or personal problem?

Could there be a medical, behavioral, or personal problem causing or significantly contributing to the performance discrepancy?

This is obviously a very delicate area. If, either through self-disclosure or behavior observation, you know or think that a medical, behavioral, or personal problem is causing or significantly contributing to the performance discrepancy, it is imperative that you stick to your role as performance manager and avoid playing amateur diagnostician.

Avoiding the problem or playing amateur diagnostician are two common mistakes managers make. Managers may avoid the problem because they do not know what to do, or for fear that they will make matters worse. In playing amateur diagnostician managers want to help the individual and think they are doing so by dispensing advice that they are not qualified to give. Even if they were qualified, such advice, if followed, could come back to bite them. "Cut me some slack, I did what you said I should do." The way you help the individual is to set performance expectations; continue to insist on desired performance; make performance matter; and, encourage the individual to get proper professional assistance.

Because of the individual's desire to continue to hold the current position or to continue to be employed, the work environment provides an excellent foundation for the individual to address whatever medical, behavioral, or personal problem that may exist. The desire to continue working motivates the individual to: a) realize that a problem exists; b) be motivated to do something about it; and, c) take prudent action to seek out and use proper professional assistance in resolving their issue or issues.

If your organization has an employee assistance program, it can serve as a valuable resource for any individual who may be experiencing any such medical, behavioral, or personal problems to take advantage of.

If the individual is getting professional help, your role is not to probe into the details of such help, but again to stick to your role as performance manager. It behooves the individual however to arrange to provide you as the manager with general information regarding cooperation and prognosis from any professionals providing assistance so that you might factor such input into your managing of the performance discrepancy.

Deciding

Having done quality thinking, and perhaps interacting, working through the performance analysis logic, you may be ready to zero in on the cause or causes of the performance discrepancy, and what to do about it.

In so doing, work through the following questions:

Most Likely Cause

Based on your analysis, what do you think is the most likely cause, or causes, of the performance discrepancy?

Alternative Solutions

Based on what you determined the most likely cause or causes to be, what are some rational potential solutions that might address the causation of the performance discrepancy?

Best Solution

Which solution, or combination of solutions, best addresses the most likely cause of causes of the performance discrepancy?

Stage 4: Implementing

Formulating an Action Plan

Having identified the most likely cause or causes of the performance discrepancy, you now need to think through just how you plan to take action to resolve the problem.

The rigor of your action plan will depend on the importance and complexity of the performance discrepancy. But regardless, you need to think through the sequence of steps, who needs to be involved in the intelligence gathering and decision making, and the timing. You also need to think about any implementation challenges that might exist and how you plan to deal with such challenges.

Constructive Communications

Communicating with the individual(s) about the performance discrepancy obviously needs to be a part of any action plan. Having quality communications regarding the performance discrepancy is a vital part of successfully resolving the performance discrepancy. Consequently, you need to devote some quality thinking to plan your communications. The performance analysis logic you worked through will be of great benefit in planning and implementing constructive communications.

The *3-Step Constructive Conflict Resolution Process* shown below provides a useful model to help guide you through having a collaborative conversation regarding resolving conflict, such as resolving performance discrepancies.

Figure 5.14 Three-Step Conflict Resolution Process

The three steps for having a viable constructive conversation to resolve conflict are:

1. Seek to understand each other.
2. What's possible?
3. Next steps.

In *seeking to understand* it is important to use assertive communication in discussing the performance discrepancy. Assertive communication is direct, clear, positive, respectful communication. Your intent is to assure that the individual understands precisely what the performance discrepancy is and why it is important.

You have a better chance of achieving such understanding by using assertive communication, so called "I messages", than by using aggressive communications, or so called "You messages", which are most times perceived as an attack. Although there are situations, such as with repeat offenders or serious violations, when aggressive communications may be called for.

You also want to provide an opportunity for the individual to give his or her side of the story and perhaps attempt to "explain away" their misconduct or failure to perform up to expectations when it is not an ability deficiency. When it comes time for the individual to speak it is important that you be attentive and seek to understand just what is being said. This does not mean that you need to agree with what they are saying, or condone their actions.

The amount of maneuverability afforded in the *"what's possible?"* step will depend on the specific performance discrepancy you are dealing with and what stage you are at in taking possible management action. In some cases, you need to be firm as to what has to happen. In other cases, there may be some room to discuss possible alternatives.

But regardless of how directive or non-directive the approach called for, if you adopt the mental model that your goal is *to help the individual help him or herself* and not to punish, you will be more likely to do the right thing. This is true even when disciplinary action is called for. You are taking such action to arrange appropriate external consequences to help the individual understand what is going and to takr prudent action to resolve the discrepancy. And you are doing so because the requisite self-management did not work. If the individual does not take advantage of the *positive discipline* prescribed to help them help themselves, they are in essence discharging him or herself if it comes to that. The individual most likely will not see it this way. At least at the time.

Stage 5. Learning from Experience

At an appropriate time, or times, during your attempt to analyze and resolve the performance discrepancy, do some reflective thinking to capture what you have learned from the experience.

Call a personal time out and do some quality thinking and self-observation around such questions as those listed below.

In my attempt to analyze and resolve this performance discrepancy:

"What did I/we do well?"

"What worked particularly well?"

"What could have been improved?"

"What specifically would I/we do differently if I had to do it all over again?"

"How can I/we apply what was learned in the future?"

The performance analysis logic described is a practical and proven tool to help you do quality thinking, interacting, and take resultant action to analyze and resolve performance discrepancies. It allows you to take a logical, focused approach to resolve a performance problem rather than trying different things in the hopes that one might stick.

The process described is most assuredly the most comprehensive you will run across. In fact, initially it may seem to be a little overwhelming. It may seem like cracking a walnut with a sledge hammer. But rest assured, once you become accustomed to using the logic you will become confident and comfortable in using the process to analyze and resolve performance discrepancies where the answers on how to best proceed are not obvious.

Appendix A contains a case study, the Alex Reed case, to help you practice applying the performance analysis logic.

6. BUILDING BLOCK #4: TEAMS: SYNERGY AT WORK

Alone we can do so little.
Together we can do so much.

—Helen Keller

Applying the concepts, structures, tools, and techniques discussed thus far will provide you with the requisite clarity, confidence, and competence to optimize the contributions and potential of individuals working for you. Working with them to build high-performing teams is the next level. Doing so will allow you to increase effectiveness and efficiency in attaining desired results exponentially.

> Teams should be able to act with the same unity of purpose and focus as a well-motivated individual.
>
> —Bill Gates

The purpose of this chapter is to equip you with the capability to meet the Bill Gates challenge as voiced above.

Why Teams?

Fierce competition, technological advances, cost management, information technology, heightened customer expectations, and the rapidity of change have created a heightened interest in teams, teamwork, and team structures, processes and tools. Increasingly organizations are looking to teams as a critical strategy to improve quality, speed, flexibility, productivity, customer service, and cost effectiveness. Teams have become the basic organizational building blocks.

Some reasons why teams can make organizational sense are listed below.[1]

- More people in the organization share leadership.
- More experience and knowledge brought to bear on complex problems.
- More information goes directly to the point where action can be taken.
- More decisions are effectively and quickly executed because implementers have been part of the decision-making process.
- More people view themselves as being able to contribute to the success of the business by striving for a common purpose.
- More innovation and risk taking is possible because there is a higher level of trust among members of the team.
- More people are listening to their customers and have authority to solve customer issues and concerns.
- More people focus on learning from mistakes rather than unproductive competition.
- More strategic planning and thinking takes place because as the team makes more day-to-day decisions, their leaders and managers have more time for higher level work and adding greater value.

What Is a "Team"

Team: A small number of people having complementary knowledge and skills working collaboratively toward a unifying purpose using common processes and tools and holding themselves individually and mutually accountable for achieving shared aspirations.

Just calling a group a team does not make it one. There is a lot more to it than that. A group has to work hard to become a team and to sustain itself as a team. Transforming into a team requires commitment, know-how, and discipline. And organizations need to sanction and nurture such transformations if teams are going to be successful on any large scale.

Let us not confuse teams and teamwork. All organizations and organizational groups stand to benefit from effective teamwork. That is, people getting along, cooperating, effectively communicating, and helping each other out when and as needed. You can have effective teamwork without the formal deployment of teams. But, you cannot have effective teams without good teamwork.

Teams are not for everyone. Just as with any organizational form, the use of teams has to fit the situation.

There are two primary reasons teams are not for all situations.

1. The organization, be it the organization as a whole or specific organizational units, is not ready.

2. The organizational structure, the nature of the work, or work processes does not warrant.

The greater the degree of *interdependence* required amongst the people doing the work, the greater the chance that teams will be beneficial. An organization must evaluate if there is sufficient task interdependence in a group or groups before moving to deploy teams. A sales organization for example with sales representatives spread over a wide territory would undoubtedly benefit from good teamwork, with the sales representatives sharing information and results on a periodic basis. But trying to turn such an organization into a team and sustain it as such would probably not be worth the time and effort.

Types of Teams

Teams can be used for accomplishing both ongoing and time-limited results. Listed below are the different types of organizational teams.

Figure 6.1 Types of Teams

Type	Purpose
Ongoing Teams	
• **Natural work groups**	To effectively and efficiently live the identity and achieve the direction of an organizational unit.
• **Coordinating teams**	To develop strategic direction and align, coordinate, and integrate the diverse activities of the organization as a whole or specific organizational units or major organizational projects. Executive and leadership teams are examples of coordinating teams.
Time-Limited Teams (ad-hoc; project teams)	
• **New product teams**	To develop and launch a new product or service.

- **Improvement teams**   To make recommendations and perhaps implement such recommendations for solving important problems, improving operations, or developing or streamlining work processes.

- **Task teams**   To implement defined specific actions.

There are two other team labels that need to be discussed: *cross-functional teams* and *self-directed teams*. These labels refer not to the type of team so much as how it is constituted, managed, or operates.

Cross-functional teams

A cross-functional team is a description of the composition of the team. The team is composed of people from different parts of the organization or different functions. The idea is to get a diverse group of people together who are knowledgeable regarding the opportunity or challenge and let their collective wisdom go to work. Cross-functional teams can be either ongoing in nature, such as a committee, or time-limited, such as the types of teams listed above.

Self-directed teams

Self-directed describes how a team is designed to operate. The term relates to the structure of a team and the autonomy allowed to perform its work.

Self-directed teams, when used, are typically used for natural work groups. Such teams report to a manager but plan, perform, and control their day-to-day work with little supervision.

A common practice in using the self-directed team form of governance for natural work groups is to rotate the leadership role from within the group every so often, such as every six months. The group still needs a point person to drive their work processes and assure effective team meetings. In its early stages of a team's development, it may be appropriate for the supervising manager to be a part of the team and participate in its operational business. As the team matures, it most likely will be appropriate for a supervisor to move outside of the specific operations of a team and be available as a resource, trainer, and coach for the team, when and as needed.

An example of a successful implementation of this form of governance was in a city I worked with that transitioned to the way it did business to allow the three maintenance groups in the city to plan, perform, and control their daily work rather than be directed by three frontline managers. They would meet on a weekly basis to schedule their work. Then the first thing each morning to make any scheduling and equipment usage adjustments. The superintendent was available to provide direction, guidance, and support when and as needed.

Stages of Team Development

All teams begin as immature groups *(The Forming Stage)*.[2] This is especially true for time-limited teams as compared with natural work groups whose members have already know each other and have shared common work experiences. At this stage team members are trying to get a feel regarding just what this kind of team is all about, the nature of its work, and how they fit in?

The group needs to determine its identity and direction, how it is going to conduct its work, respective roles and responsibilities, how it is going to meet and communicate, and how problems are going to be resolved and decisions made *(The Storming Stage)*. There is ample room here for disagreement and conflict. It is important for the team to realize that such struggles are inevitable. It is also critical for the team to realize that conflict is not something to be avoided. Rather, disagreements are something to be welcomed, as long as it is constructive conflict and not destructive conflict. That is, people collaborating to seek to understand one another and optimize their decision-making.

Realizing that differences are inevitable and that constructive conflict is to be welcomed, the team establishes guidelines and processes for resolving conflict, making decisions, communications, and handling change *(The Norming Stage)*. If successfully managed, it is at this stage that the group can experience a breakthrough and start to be worthy of calling itself a team.

The team has learned how to be a team. There is agreement on its identity, direction, and the rules of engagement. Members are aligned toward achieving results and the team is making significant progress *(The Performing Stage)*.

For time-limited teams there is a fifth stage–*The Adjournment Stage*. In this stage the team's time-limited purpose is completed and the team is broken up.

Characteristics of High-Performing Teams

As previously stated, forming a high-performing team, be it an ongoing or time-limited team is no easy task. And it is an ongoing task requiring commitment, know-how, and discipline. It takes work to evolve and sustain such a team. If you are committed to building a high-performing team there is a good chance that you will get there using the proper structure, processes, and tools. But be forewarned, that it is no easy task. And teams can be fragile, so you need to be on constant alert.

The model on the following pages provides you with a practical and proven model for developing high-performing teams. It keys in on the main characteristics for building high-performing teams. Use it as a guide in doing so.

Figure 6.2 Characteristics of High-Performing Teams

BUILDING BLOCKS	DESCRIPTION
RESULTS	Develop shared aspirations and assure understanding, acceptance, and commitment amongst all team members.
ACCOUNTABILITY	Ensure that both individuals and the team as a whole answer for their actions. Everyone needs to adhere to the commitments the team has made as a whole and to one another.
COLLABORATION	Engage in open, genuine, skillful, and timely dialogue in going about the business of the team.
TRUST	Develop understood and accepted expectations and engage in appropriate resultant behaviors that lead to a shared belief that team members will act in the best interest of the team and one another. Be comfortable with being authentic and vulnerable with one another. In so doing, building an environment of psychological safety for team members.

Building Block	Applicable Structures Helpful Mechanisms Effective Interactions

RESULTS	For the organization as a whole and organizational entities:
	• Develop shared aspirations around Identity and Direction.
	   IDENTITY: Purpose and Core Values
	   DIRECTION: Workable Vision Strategic Path Actions
	• Identify measures of success.
	• Monitor and modify progress.
	• Have meaningful strategy meetings.
	
	For coordinating teams, such as leadership teams:
	• Draft Charter.
	• Draft Team Agreements.
	• Monitor and modify progress.
	
	For time-limited (ad hoc) teams:
	• Identify Project Sponsor.
	• Draft Project Charter
	• Draft Action (or Project) Plan.
	• Draft Team Agreements.
	• Monitor and modify progress.

ACCOUNTABILITY	• Define team roles. • Clarify authorities. • Support and constructively challenge one another. • Recognize and celebrate team successes. • Assess how well team is working together and identify areas for improvement.
COLLABORATION	• Use sound processes to catalyze quality thinking and interacting. • Use the appropriate decision-making mode, that is, unilateral, voting, consultative, or consensus, to fit the situation. • Encourage and respect divergent points of view. • Seek to understand one another. • Work on projects together when and as feasible. • Plan for and conduct productive meetings.

TRUST	• Be authentic. • Understand, appreciate, and utilize each other's unique differences. • Be consistent. • Be willing to be vulnerable. • Be willing to take risks. • Be non-judgmental and non-critical. • In in providing constructive feedback, focus on the results or behavior, not on the person. • Deliver on commitments. • Support one another.

Notes: Applicable Structures, Helpful Mechanisms, and Effective Interactions

- The Trust building block is shown as the foundation of the model, with the other building blocks feeding into it. It is depicted this way because trust is not something that is quickly built. Rather, it is built on the quality and frequency of relationships. Trust is built by a team effectively working through the other three building blocks together to achieve tangible results that are meaningful.

- With regard to ongoing teams, my book, *Making and Fulfilling Your Dreams as a Leader*,[3] provides requisite concepts, structures, processes, and tools for a leader or leadership team to do quality thinking and interacting to craft both the ongoing and time-limited results for an organization or organizational unit to be successful.

  In addition to being a part of *Making and Fulfilling Your Dreams as a Leader*, crafting and using project or action plans is a part of chapter 4, *Clarity: Developing Shared Expectations*, in this book.

- Specific team tools, for both ongoing and time-limited teams, are covered later in this chapter.

- Every team project needs a *Project Sponsor*. A project sponsor most times is the individual or group who initiated or commissioned the project. When the team members are all from the same organizational unit, the project sponsor is the organizational unit leader. This is the individual or group the team can turn to when and as needed for support. *When the team is comprised of members from different organizational units, it is imperative that a project sponsor be named at the outset of the project.*

- A *Team Charter* summarizes why the team was created. It is typically a one or two-page document defining the purpose, desired outcomes, and accountability of a coordinating or time-limited team. A team charter is crafted by following the first step in formulating a project or action plan, that is, defining Project Specifications, as described in Chapter 4, *Clarity: Developing Shared Expectations*.

    The role of the project sponsor should be summarized in the Accountability section of the Project Specifications.

- *Team Agreements* are discussed below.

Team Agreements[4]

Regardless of the project planning rigor needed for a project, it is important to create agreements amongst the key team players or, as applicable, the entire team relative to the necessary *commitments* that need to be made to one another to ensure project success. It is also important to determine the *mutual accountabilities* that need to be followed to assure that such commitments are honored.

BUILDING BLOCK #4: TEAMS: SYNERGY AT WORK

Team Agreements   Principles and ideas the leader and team members deem essential to allow them to effectively work together and to manage the work to be done.

Creating and living team agreements helps the team leader ensure that the team is working productively together. *Team agreements are applicable to ongoing teams, such as leadership teams, as well as time-limited teams, such as project teams.*

Team agreements are analogous to the core values of the organization as a whole or an organizational unit. Both need to be few in number, critical to success, and lived. The distinctions are that whereas core values are essential and enduring beliefs to guide everyday behavior of the organization as a whole, or an organizational unit; team agreements are commitments the leader and team member make to one another regarding principles and ideas they hold to be important in managing team member relationships and the work of the team.

In his best-selling book, *Principles*[5], Ray Dalio, founder of Bridgewater, a large hedge fund organization, espouses the importance of principles to live and work by. His message to leaders is that they need to operate by principles that are so clearly laid out that their logic can easily be assessed by the leader and others to determine if they are walking the talk.

Listed below are three questions recommended by Allan McCarthy that are helpful in creating team agreements.

In creating team agreements with your team, consider these three questions:

1. Think of the *characteristics of great teams* that you know of, or been a part of. List those characteristics that promoted success.

2. Given your knowledge and experience with successful teams, and your knowledge of this team, what are *the key agreements you think are most important for this team to manage its team dynamics?*

3. How should the team members go about *holding each other accountable for each agreement?* If the team or team member is not following the agreement, how is the situation constructively handled?

Below are a few samplings of some team agreements from various teams. These are meant to be samplings only, and not meant to be copied. While it is not necessarily a bad thing to borrow other's thoughts on formulating team agreements, any adapting must be taken with careful thought to assure that the agreements are consistent with the voice and convictions of the team leader and team members, and the work of the team.

- Create a safe place where team members can express divergent points of view openly and passionately without fear of being ridiculed. Constructive conflict needs to be encouraged, not discouraged. Doing so allows for better decision making and understanding.

  Accountability: Speak up if and when you feel invalidated. We need to clear up such situations when they occur. Also, we need to periodically discuss just how rigorous our transparency really is.

- Have growth mindsets, not fixed mindsets. Need to be willing and able to change our mental models based upon new knowledge and experiences.

  Accountability: Question each other when we sense someone is being mired in a fixed mindset. Why are they thinking that way?

- Come to team meetings prepared to discuss any items on the agenda, what is going on with regard to your project responsibilities, and any action items you have been assigned in previous meetings.

    Accountability: Call each other out on "ball dropping" without getting emotional and accusatory.

- At the end of each team meeting, agree on conclusions, actions to be taken, and what is to be and not to be communicated outside the meeting, as well as the timing and individual responsibilities regarding any such communication.

    Accountability: Start each meeting with feedback regarding agreed-to conclusions and actions to be taken from previous meetings, as well as related communications outside the meeting relative to such topics.

Listed below are the agreements Ray Dalio found to be most important in working with his teams:

1. Put our honest thoughts on the table.
2. Have thoughtful disagreements in which people are willing to shift their opinions as they learn.
3. Have agreed-upon ways of deciding, for example, voting, having clear authorities, if disagreements remain so that we can move beyond them without resentments.

These samplings should provide you with a good understanding of what team agreements are, their importance, and how powerful they can be.

Team Roles

For intact or natural work group teams roles and responsibilities need to be clear. The position planning logic discussed in chapter

4, *Clarity, Developing Shared Expectations,* provides a practical and proven planning logic for defining the role and set of results a position and those reporting to it is organized to achieve.

For both time-limited teams and intact groups operating as self-directed teams, it is important to define specific roles at the outset.

For such teams, Figure 6.3 below lists some of the possible roles, both outside and inside the core team.

Figure 6.3 Possible Roles: Time-Limited and Self-Directed Teams

Roles Outside the Core Team

Role	Who	Responsibilities
Leadership Support	People in higher management who sanction the use of teams.	Establish and maintain a positive, supportive environment to allow teams to excel. Ensure that teams have the required clarity of direction, skill mix, information, training, authority, and resources.
Project Sponsor	A specific person (or people) in management who sanctions a time-limited team and to whom the team can turn to as needed.	Provides ongoing guidance and support including helping the team manage organizational and boundary issues as required.
Staff Support	Specialists outside the core team who may be called on to help the team periodically by providing data, resources, and training	Provide understood and appropriate advice and service to the team as requested. It is important that Leadership Support or the Project Sponsor assure that team support people are identified and willing and able to provide support to the team when and as needed.

Roles Inside the Core Team

Role	Who	Responsibilities
Team Leader	Elected or appointed team member who guides the team.	• Coordinate the work of the team. • Conduct team meetings. • Serve as spokesperson for the team. • Follow-up on actions to be taken.
Key Result Area (KRA) Leaders	If it fits the team's business, individual team members responsible for taking the lead relative to the Key Result Areas the team identified in defining its business.	• Take the lead for the specific KRA assigned. • Lead discussions at team meetings for the specific KRA. • Coordinate action to be taken and track progress for the particular KRA.
Team Recorder	A team member who keeps a visible record of the team's business (the "Team Memory").	• Record at meetings the team's decisions and actions to be taken and, summarize at end of meeting. • When appropriate, record team ideas, data, and so forth on a flipchart or whiteboard to assure understanding and to help the team track what is going on.
Team Facilitator	A team member or a person outside the team called upon to help the team with its team meeting or specific process such as how are we going to go about solving this problem, make this decision, plan a course of action, and so forth.	Manages team process to help assure effective and efficient outcomes and full participation.
Team Member	Individual contributors on the team.	Actively participate, provide ideas, share responsibility, support other team members, and perform the work of the team.

Team Meetings

The word "meeting" often creates a negative reaction for people in the work world. A common perception is that having to attend a meeting takes one away from doing "real work". Such negativity is understandable considering the number of meetings most people have attended that did need to be held in the first place, were poorly planned or conducted, did not have the right people present, or did not produce effective results.

An unnecessary or poorly planned or conducted meeting is a time waster and consequently expensive. Poor meeting management is also inconsiderate when you think of the time imposition placed on those attending the meeting.

But meetings are not bad or good. They just are. When properly planned and conducted, meetings can be extremely effective and a good use of everyone's time. Meetings are important to a team because that is where it conducts the bulk of its business.

Tips for Productive Team Meetings

- Realize that there are different types of meetings for different purposes. There are regularly scheduled team meetings; "check-in" meetings; and ad-hoc meetings to work on specific planning, strategy, issues, or decisions. Consequently, the objective of the meeting and its design need to be crafted to optimize its effectiveness and efficiency.

- Determine who needs to attend the meeting.

- Create the agenda. For recurring meetings, recommend that a meeting template comprised of the major discussion area for such meetings be established. Specific items for each component can then be identified at the outset of the meeting or in advance.

- Let participants know what if anything they need to do in advance to prepare for the meeting.

- Conduct an organized meeting.

    - Have clear roles.

    - Agree on team meeting guidelines to capture desired key participant behaviors before, during, and after team meetings. Assure that participants adhere to these guidelines.

    - Arrange for active participation by all team members.

    - Designate a person to be the recorder to keep track of team *Decisions* and *Actions to Be Taken* (What? Who? When?). Also have the recorder keep track of *"Parking Lot"* items. That is, items that came up in the meeting but for whatever reason did not get discussed, but should be.

    - If the meeting is a follow-on to previous meetings include a follow-up to any *Actions to Be Taken* as part of the agenda.

    - Consider having someone serve as a facilitator when the team is working on an important issue. This frees up the leader up to concentrate on content rather than process.

    - Decide on the process to be used when working on an important issue. Consider having someone record what is going on a flipchart or white board to serve as the "team memory."

- Before adjourning, have the recorder summarize the *Decisions Made* and *Actions to Be Taken* items recorded. Clarify any differences in understanding before adjourning. Also, before adjourning, decide on any *Communications Needed Outside the Meeting*. Specifically, what do we need to communicate; who, is going to make the communicates; and, when and how the communications should occur. Also agree on anything that needs to stay in the meeting.

- Start and end on time, and insist that participants adhere to this practice.

Collaborative Decision-Making

Effective collaboration is essential if a group is to perform as a team. Collaboration is one of the four building blocks in the *Characteristics of a High-Performing Team* model described in Figure 6.2 on pages 169-171. When the team is effectively collaborating, it is engaging in open, genuine, skillful, and timely dialogue in going about its business.

To achieve effective collaboration, a team needs to strive to develop a culture built on:

- Inclusiveness.
- Full participation.
- Shared responsibility.
- Being authentic and vulnerable with one another.
- Seeking to understand one another.
- Respecting different points of view.
- Encouraging constructive conflict.

The team uses constructive conflict, as contrasted with destructive conflict, as a key component for making effective decisions. And in so doing, building trust. Constructive conflict is about team members feeling okay about expressing their various points of view in a respectful, objective manner. The focus, both in terms of expression and reaction, is on the idea, not the person. Destructive conflict on the other hand is typically rooted in relationships and winning and losing.

Teams that have developed trust amongst its members will actually look for opportunities to disagree on important issues. Team members may argue vehemently and passionately about such issues. But they will do so constructively with an aim toward optimizing the team's decision-making effectiveness, not to grandstand or to win.

Team Decision-Making Modes

There are various decision-making modes a team can use: unilateral; majority vote; consultative; and consensus as shown below.

Figure 6.4 Team Decision-Making Modes

Unilateral	One person decides for the team.
Majority Vote	Half plus one vote is the decision for the team.
Consultative	Team leader or primary decision maker taps into individual team members or the team as a whole to help make the best decision.
Consensus	The team leader or primary decision maker joins the in making the decision. Everyone is on equal footing. Team members agree that regardless of the decision, they will each support it.

The team leader or primary decision maker needs to weigh the situational variables when choosing a decision-making mode. The importance of the decision; the acceptance of the decision; who possesses the requisite knowledge; the degree of decision-making latitude afforded the team; and, the time available are the key situational variables. The leader or primary decision maker should inform the team of the mode to be used in making a specific decision.

Each decision-making mode has its advantages and disadvantages. The spirit of collaboration needs to be a constant regardless of the mode used. The consultative and consensus modes by their nature invite a much greater degree of collaboration than either the unilateral or majority vote modes. Consultative and consensus are the shared decision-making modes.

Summarizing the advantages and disadvantages of each decision-making mode:

The *unilateral mode* can be fast, clear, and decisive. It can be an appropriate mode for issues that: are minor; have to be made immediately; or that the team leader or primary decider is definite about the way the decision should go, and possesses the requisite knowledge to make an effective decision. This mode may be appropriate when there is not much leeway for the team to make a decision or does not possess the requisite knowledge to make an informed decision. Obviously, this mode does not afford much room for collaboration. But the team leader or primary decision maker is most times best served by sharing the rationale behind the decision.

Majority vote can also be fast and decisive. Unless arranged for, this mode does not allow for quality give and take before making the decision. Majority vote results in winners and losers.

On important decisions, the team leader or primary decider who wants to make the final decision but is open to various inputs can be helped significantly in making an effective decision by using the *consultative mode* and tapping into individual team members or the team as a whole. The reason for tapping into the group is to make a better decision; not to make anyone feel better. This is extremely important. Team member support for the decision will most likely increase if the members feel that they were genuinely engaged in having the opportunity to input into the decision. The consultative mode is obviously more time consuming than unilateral decision making and majority vote. Skill on the part of the team leader or primary decider is also needed to optimize the benefits of this mode.

The *consensus mode* can be very time consuming and consequently should be used sparingly. But this mode can be beneficial when used for decisions when the team leader or primary decider is faced with an important decision and can live with any decision the team comes up with. This mode provides for the greatest degree of team member ownership. People tend to own things they help create.

When using the consensus mode, the team leader or primary decider can always fall back and use the consultative mode if the team cannot reach a decision. The team leader must realize however in using the consensus mode that teams, especially those that are not experienced in using this mode, will most times struggle. That is the nature of the beast.

Collaborative Decision-Making Process

Collaboration is the act or process of shared discovery or creation. It is about a team working effectively together to get different views out on the table, having effective dialogue regarding the respective merits of each, and coming to a proper resolution.

The process outlined below can be used by a team on a repeatable basis to facilitate collaborative decision making. It is applicable when the team uses the shared decision-making modes, that is, the consultative and consensus modes. Various team tools that have been discussed, as well as additional tools to be discussed shortly in this chapter, can be used when and as appropriate to enhance the shared decision-making process.

Figure 6.5 Collaborative Decision-Making Process

1. Clarify purpose	• *"Why are we getting together?"* • *"What is the decision to be made?"* • *"What are we trying to accomplish?"*
2. Get divergent inputs and views	• *"Who needs to be involved?"* • *Create a shared pool of information.* • *Expect some confusion because of all the different information generated.* • *There is no need to be in agreement at this phase.* • *Record comments, issues, and concerns.* • *"Go slow to go fast." Quality time spent here will pay big dividends later.*
3. Seek to understand	• *Build a shared understanding of divergent views and perspectives.* • *Use effective communication skills.*
4. Identify options	• *"What are the viable options or alternatives?"* • *"Can we create new options by connecting different views and perspectives?"*
5. Make a decision	• *"How are we going to decide?"* • *"What is the best option or alternative?"*
6. Take action	• *"How are we going to implement this decision?"* • *"What?" "Who?" "When?"*

Testing for Agreement

As a team leader you are naturally concerned as to what team members are thinking or feeling regarding key issues being discussed or decided.

Methods for testing for agreement are outlined below. The importance of the decision and its acceptance should dictate which consensus testing method is most appropriate.

Figure 6.6 Testing for Agreement

Speculate	Speculate that it seems that consensus has been reached. Observe the reaction to the statement. Invite feedback.
Individual Polling	Ask each team member if she or he can support the decision being proposed.
Gradients of Agreement Scale	Poll the team using the Gradients of Agreement methodology described below.

The *Gradients of Agreement Scale*[6] is an extremely effective way to poll the team to determine the degree of support for a proposed important decision before it is implemented.

The Gradients of Agreement Scale allows the leader to specifically assess the degree of support that exists for implementing the decision. If adequate support exists, the leader can feel confident that the decision will be effectively implemented. If adequate support for the decision does not exist, the process allows the leader and team to identify specific implementation concerns and barriers. Given such input the leader can assess if the decision needs to be reframed or if implementation strategies need to be revised. Or whether the decision should be postponed or scrapped.

BUILDING COMMITMENT

How to Use

1. Clearly state the proposal or decision.

2. Use the scale below to poll each team member. Change the wording if you wish. Replicate the scale on a flipchart or white board.

Gradients of Agreement Scale

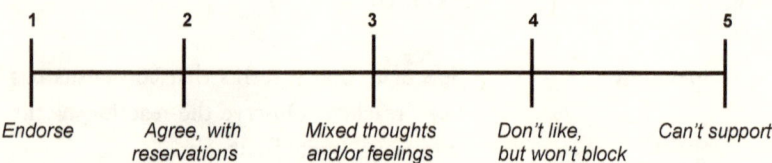

The scale is a way to get beyond simple "yes" or "no" statements of support such as the individual polling method described above. "Yes" and "no" can have many different meanings. Using the scale makes it easier for group members to be honest and specific about their thoughts and feelings regarding the proposed decision. In addition, members can register less than whole hearted support without fearing that their statement will be interpreted as a veto.

3. Decide how to take the poll.

    Options:
    - Each individual gives rating and says why. No discussion.
    - Show of hands working down the scale.
    - Simultaneous declaration. Write down number and hold up.
    - Secret ballot.

The first option combined with a second round makes for an especially effective process in that individuals may want to change their voting after hearing others rationale on how why they voted the way they did.

4. Record the results on the flipchart or white board using the scale shown above.

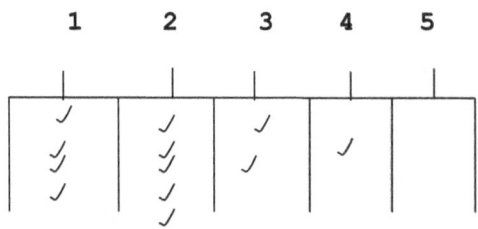

5. As the leader, determine your degree of comfort with the outcome to assure effective execution of the decision. If not, you may want to reframe the proposal or decision, revise implementation strategies, or postpone or scrap the decision.

Team Learning

A team needs to call periodic "time outs" to assess how well it is working together; what it is accomplishing; as called for, make necessary improvements and adjustments; and, to celebrate.

Areas of focus for team time outs include the following:

Team Process

"How well are we working together?"
"What's working well?"
"What needs improvement?"

Work Accomplishments

"What have been our most significant work accomplishments?"
"What have we learned from these accomplishments that we can use in moving forward?"
"Where have we fallen short, and what are we going to do about it?"

Project Work

At the completion of a significant project or at milestone events along the way, assess how the project is going, both in terms of accomplishments and process. Also assess what the team has learned, what improvements or adjustments need to be made, and what needs to be replicated on future projects.

Team Tools

Team tools are used to facilitate and make more effective and efficient the team's collaboration and decision making.

On the following pages are some of the tools that teams find quite useful.

Several of these tools, such as Goal Analysis, Preconditions, Goal Analysis, Problem Analysis, Decision-Making Framework, Decision Analysis, and Action (or Project) Planning, are demonstrated in this book.

Tool	Page
Gap Analysis	190
Preconditions	191
Goal Analysis	192
Problem Analysis	194
Decision-Making Framework	200
Decision Making	202
Pros and Cons	202
Decision Analysis	204
Mindmapping	207
Fishbone Diagram	213
Functional Process Mapping	216
Narrowing the Number of Alternatives	218
Multivoting	218
Nominal Group Technique	220
Action (or Project) Planning	222

BUILDING COMMITMENT

GAP ANALYSIS

What It Is

Gap analysis is a broad planning tool. The tool starts with defining the Desired Future State and the Current State. The differences between these two states constitute the "Gap". Obstacles in the way of closing the gap and options and strategies to do so are then identified in completing this quick and effective planning model.

When to Use

There is a need to engage in quality thinking and interacting regarding moving things to a new and better place.

How to Use

1. Define the Objective.
2. Define the characteristics of the Desired Future State. Goal Analysis or the Affinity Diagram, discussed in the following pages, are ideal tools for doing so.
3. Define the characteristics of the Current State.
4. Identify the Obstacles that must be overcome and the Options to close the gap.
5. Weighing the various options, determine the best Strategies to move from the Current State to the Future Desired State.

Objective: _____

Current State → THE GAP → Desired Future State

Obstacles → Options → Strategies

PRECONDITIONS

What It Is

Specifying preconditions is a quick but important check to identify any important "GIVENS" that may exist relating to your decision or project. Identifying the preconditions up front minimizes the chances of "wheel spinning" and "second guessing" and the undesirable effects of each.

Categories of Preconditions

Commitments	What, if any, are the commitments or promises that you or others have made that have a bearing on your decision?
Resource Limitations	What, if any, resource limitations, that is, time, money, people involvement, and so forth, exist that have a bearing on your decision?

When to Use

At the outset of a decision or project, once your decision objective or project objective has been properly defined.

How to Use

Identify any important commitments and resource limitations that may exist.

GOAL ANALYSIS[7]

What It Is

The goal analysis technique provides a practical and proven way to move from abstract language to more specific language when needed. You do so by focusing on your objective or goal and citing specific evidences of success. In other words: "How do you know success when you see it"?

When to Use

When you need to translate abstract language (*"fuzzies"*) into specific or concrete terms before you can effectively proceed.

For example, an objective "to improve the safety consciousness of division operation and maintenance employees" leaves a lot of room for interpretation. What you would want to do is ask: *"How do you know good safety consciousness when you see it?"* That is, what is the target group doing when they are behaving in a "safety conscious" manner? Once you know the answer to this question in specific, behavioral terms you can more effectively and efficiently proceed with your decision making.

The goal analysis technique was cited on page 63 as an excellent tool to craft desired outcomes for a key result area objective in applying the position planning logic.

How to Use

1. Write down the **GOAL** or objective. Most people use goal and objective interchangeably. I use goal to refer to longer range aspirations, and objective to refer to more short-term outcomes. There could be several objectives called for to achieve a specific goal.

2. **JOT** down in words and phrases the evidences that, if achieved, would cause you to say that the goal was successful met.

3. **SORT** out the jottings into logical categories or clusters.

4. **LABEL** each cluster. Develop a "header" (just a word or two) for each cluster that summarizes the cluster.

5. **EXPAND** each label into a statement that captures the essence of the ideas expressed in the cluster, that is, the jottings. Mentally preface each statement with the word "when", in that the statements represent the conditions that exist *when* the goal (objective) is achieved.

6. **TEST** the list of criteria. "If all of these criteria were being met, would I say the goal was being successfully met?" If the answer is "no", determine what is missing. If the answer is "yes", your goal analysis is complete.

Note:

The use of Goal Analysis as a useful mechanism is recommended in Chapter 3, Clarity: Developing Shared Expectations, to facilitate quality thinking in generating and sorting out Desired Outcomes for a position's Key Result Areas.

In Chapter 4, Clarity: Developing Shared Expectations, Goal Analysis is recommended as a useful mechanism to craft Desired Outcomes to meet the Project Objective in the Project Specifications step in action (or project) planning.

PROBLEM ANALYSIS[8]

What It Is

A systematic process for describing and defining a problem to determine its cause.

When to Use

The cause of the problem is not obvious. Deliberate analysis is used to identify the root cause of the problem.

How to Use

1. ***Describe*** **the problem.**

   "What SHOULD be happening?"
   "What is ACTUALLY is happening"

   The gap between the SHOULD and the ACTUAL is the problem description.

   When several related problems are occurring, subdivide into separate problems for analysis purposes. After analysis, the problems can, if appropriate, be grouped together to determine the proper resolution.

   Describe the problem in a single sentence that captures the essence of the challenge.

2. ***Define or specify*** **the problem.**

   The Is/Is Not Analysis process described below is an excellent tool for defining or specifying a problem. It is a troubleshooting tool. It catalyzes quality and critical thinking in gathering and stratifying relevant data in ways that expose underlying patterns. Discovering such patterns makes it easier to identify the root cause of the problem.

The Is/Is Not Analysis allows you to gather and sort out data to see just what information you have, And, what information you do not have, and need to gather relative to the problem.

The problem definition serves as a standard against which to test possible causes to see which cause or combination of causes best accounts for the definition or specification.

Conducting an Is/Is Not Analysis

a. Specify the problem characteristics. "What IS the problem?" Answer the questions below as they relate to the problem description. *Be precise and continue to pursue each question until you cannot break it done any further.* That is you want to "Question to a void." Not "avoid", but "a void.".

WHAT?	(Identification)	What specifically is the discrepancy? What more can be said that is not included your problem description?
WHO?	(Individual/ group)	Who is the person or group with whom you are experiencing the discrepancy?
WHERE?	(Physical or geographical location)	Where is the discrepancy seen?
WHEN?	(Occasion)	Is it a "day one" problem? Or did it occur over time?
		If it is not a "day one" problem", when did the discrepancy first occur?
		When does the discrepancy occur (specific times, tasks, activities, and so forth)?

EXTENT?	(Magnitude/ progression)	How often does the discrepancy occur (number of times, % of the time, and so forth)? Is the discrepancy becoming greater, less, or staying the same?

b. Bracket the problem characteristics by specifying "What <u>IS NOT</u> the problem that could be?"

Defining the limits of the problem allows you to contrast where the problem occurs and does not occur. Doing so allows you to identity patterns and possibly discover clues to cause.

In defining what the problem IS NOT, make the IS NOT data as close to the IS data as possible. That is, describe where the problem is not occurring although it would be reasonable to expect that it might occur there. A "tight" problem specification increases your chances of unveiling key patterns and clues to cause. You want to contrast apples to apples, and not apples to papayas.

In defining the problem, it is more effective to specify the IS and IS NOT data for a particular problem characteristic at the same time rather than to go back to the IS NOT data after specifying the IS data. Doing so will sharpen your analysis.

Before moving on, identify any additional intelligence you need to gather and any assumptions you are making that need to be checked out.

	IS *(the problem?)*	IS NOT *(the problem that could be?)*
WHAT?		
WHO?		
WHERE?		
WHEN?		
EXTENT?		

c. Contrast the IS and IS NOT data to identify patterns and possible clues to cause.

Review your IS and IS NOT specifications for each of the problem characteristics and make note of any patterns or possible clues to cause. The question you want to ask is: *"What, if anything, is unique, odd, or different about the IS and IS NOT data as it relates to the problem description"?*

IS/ IS NOT ANALYSIS FRAMEWORK

	IS (the problem?)	IS NOT (the problem that could be?)	CONTRASTS (what, if anything, is unique, odd, or different about the IS and IS NOT data?)
WHAT?			
WHO?			
WHERE?			
WHEN?			
EXTENT?			

3. **Determine the most likely cause or causes**

    Use your Is/Is Not Analysis as a guide to determine the most likely cause of causes of the problem. What clues to cause can you derive from your analysis? Which cause or causes best meet your problem specifications?

4. **Test and verify your conclusion**

Note

Is/Is Not Analysis is incorporated into the Performance Analysis model described in Chapter 5, Performance Coaching: Guiding Success.

See Appendix A, The Alex Reed Case, which demonstrates an application of Is/Is Not Analysis.

Decision-Making Framework[9]

What It Is

The decision-making framework provides an excellent context for problem solving and decision making. Specific tools such as some of those included in this *Team Tools* section can be used in the various stages of the decision-making framework.

When to Use

At the outset of problem solving and decision-making efforts that are going to require a fair amount of quality thinking and interacting.

How to Use

Work through the five stages of the framework as shown below.

THE FIVE-STAGE DECISION-MAKING FRAMEWORK

1.	**Framing**	Determining from what viewpoint the decision will be made.
2.	**Gathering Intelligence**	Gathering relevant data and inputs from appropriate sources.
3.	**Coming to Conclusions**	Making an efficient and effective decision using a systematic approach based on sound framing and good intelligence.
4.	**Implementing**	Crafting an appropriate course of action.
5.	**Learning from Experience**	Capturing both outcomes and process learning to improve efficiency and effectiveness in the future.

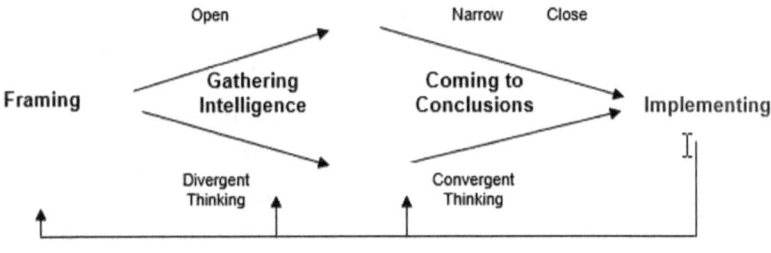

Note:

The Decision-Making Framework as well as the Is/Is Not Analysis described under the Problem Analysis tool are useful structures incorporated into the Performance Analysis Model described in chapter 5, Performance Coaching: Guiding Success.

Decision Making

There are two tools described here. One, *Pros and Cons,* is very simple and straight forward. It is a technique you are probably already familiar with. The other tool, *Decision Analysis,* is much more structured tool that is scalable to fit your application. Again, as mentioned several times previously, the art comes in using the right tool and the variability provided in applying the tool in helping you make your decision.

Pros and Cons

What It Is

Pros and cons, or advantages and disadvantages, is a simple method for evaluating a few options in deciding which one to choose. Pros and cons of each alternative are listed and discussed. This tool facilitates developing a balanced viewpoint.

When to Use

To evaluate a few alternatives to decide which to choose.

How to Use

Evaluate each alternative one at a time, listing and discussing the pros and cons of each.

	Pros	**Cons**
	+	–

Options

-

-

-

Decision Analysis[10]

What It Is

A structured process for making a decision in which each of the alternatives is evaluated against a set of decision criteria.

When to Use

For complex and important decisions where you want a high degree of reliability in the decision-making process.

How to Use

Step 1. Identify MUST Decision Criteria

If any "Go/No Go" factors, or what are often called "knockout factors", exist in making your decision, it is useful to separate your decision criteria into "MUST" and "WANT" categories.

MUST criteria, if there are any, should be kept to a minimum. They serve as a screen for eliminating alternatives that obviously do not meet any of the MUST criteria.

To be classified as a MUST criterion, the criterion needs to be:

- *Essential*
- *Reasonable*
- *Measurable*

Step 2. Identify WANT Decision Criteria

As stated above, the MUST criteria help you quickly screen out alternatives that clearly do not meet what you need. This step is extremely valuable when you indeed have MUST criteria, and you have many options.

But your real decision is made by using the WANT or decision criteria you identify.

Depending on the rigor needed you want for your decision-making process, you can assign weights to each of the criteria to differentiate their relative value in making your decision.

Step 3. Identify Alternative Solutions

Depending on the nature of the decision, generating alternative solutions may be straight forward; or it may not be. When creativity in generating alternative solutions is in order, start by brainstorming possible solutions. Then pare them down to the most viable alternatives. In other words, alternate between "thinking" and "judging". First turn on the hot water of imagination; then turn on the cold water of judgment. Using both simultaneously only produces lukewarm ideas.

Step 4. Assess Alternative Solutions

Use a Decision Matrix to assess your alternative solutions by rating them against your decision criteria.

Criteria \ Alternatives	1	2	3	4
A				
B				
C				
D				

Note:

Refer to the description of constructing and using a Decision Matrix in Chapter 3, Selection: Choosing the Right People. The application of this tool in the selection process serves as a valuable structure in determining the candidate that best meets the selection criteria.

Mindmapping

What Is It

Mindmapping is a visably interesting version of outlining. Mindmapping takes advantage of the tendency of the mind to work in short, intense "mind bursts" by allowing you to "dump" your ideas and thoughts onto paper in just a few minutes without worrying about structure or rules.

When to Use

Mindmapping is a great tool to start your thinking on any new topic. It can be used on an individual basis or when working with a group.

How to Use

1. In an oval or box in the center of a piece of paper, write down the focus of your thinking. That is, the topic you will be mindmapping.

2. Let your ideas flow from this center focus, and record the key elements around the topic in the center of the paper by using a branching technique, as shown below. Allow divergent thinking to occur.

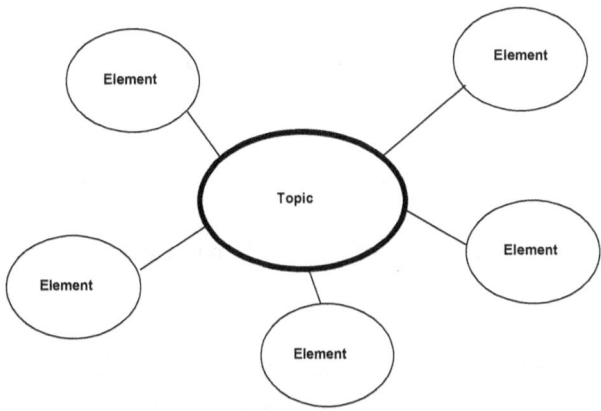

3. As you think of each element, write, in a word or two, your key ideas around that element, again using the branching technique. Do not judge or edit ideas. Writing down your ideas gets your mind "unstuck".

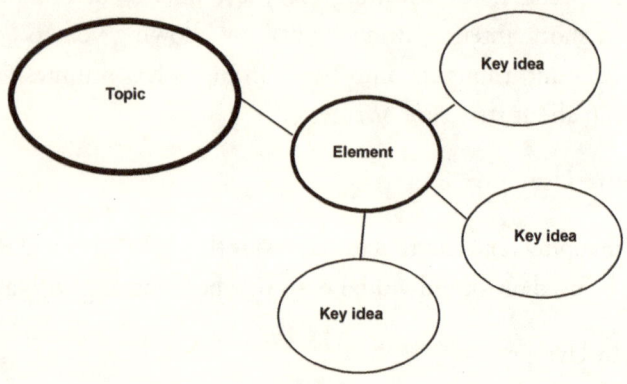

4. Continue using the branching technique until you have exhausted your "mind bursts".

5. Tidy up your mindmap as needed and use it as the foundation to catalyze and guide your thinking regarding the next logical step in your work.

Additional Tips:

- Use a large workspace to record your ideas, for example, a white board or a large sheet of paper.

- Do not be concerned about how "pretty" your mindmap looks.

- Connect related ideas from different elements by using lines and arrows.

- Consider using symbols, graphics, and color to make your mindmap come alive and increase its utility.

Affinity Diagram

What it is

The Affinity Diagram a powerful and efficient technique for generating and grouping large amounts of information in a creative and consensual manner. The advantages of the technique include: (1) creatively generating information pertinent to the challenge; (2) managing a large and possibly diverse and complex amount of information; and, (3) obtaining understanding, consensus, and commitment by all involved in the process.

The Affinity Diagram is far superior to the traditional "popcorn" type of brainstorming in that some discipline is inserted into the process and everyone is heard from. In traditional brainstorming the vocal participants often dominate and the quieter types, who may have a lot to offer, do not participate as much as they should. You will also find that you can get a lot done in a short time in using this tool.

When to Use

- To develop success criteria, desired outcomes, or decision criteria.
- To generate alternatives or options.
- To generate a list of possible opportunities or challenges.
- For developing various strategic planning statements such as core values or vision elements.

How to Use

Best used in groups of no more than 10. Subdivide into smaller groups of no more than 10 if working with a larger group. After the subgroups have completed their work, the they can discuss and consolidate their work to develop a single product. Assigning this task to representatives from each subgroup often works best in consolidating the small group products into a single product. The subgroup can report back to the larger group at a later date with their consolidation.

The Steps

1. Agree on the objective.

2. Have each member of the group silently write down her or his ideas on a Post-It notes (3" x 5"). One idea per note. Supply participants with black felt-tip pens (Sharpie pens are great) to enhance readability. Each statement should be no more than a few words, and contain a verb and a noun to minimize ambiguity.

3. After everyone has had a chance to complete their silent brainstorming, have them randomly post their notes on a large, flat surface (wall or table). Discussion at this point is limited to questions of clarification that participants may have as they scan the posted notes. Participants are encouraged to add new ideas that may be triggered by the display of group ideas.

   Recommend using large sheets of paper taped to a flat surface or laid out on a table. Use several sheets of flipchart paper if larger sheets are not available. The sheets of paper allow you to tape (Scotch tape is the best) the eventual clusters of Post-it notes for ease of transport and eventual typing.

4. In silence, participants work on grouping and regrouping similar ideas into logical clusters. Allow everyone a chance to participate. Best to limit active involvement, that is, moving notes around, to a maximum of five people at a time.

Participants can trade off. Duplications can be discarded, but only if they are exact duplications. If an idea seems to belong in more than one cluster, duplicate the note. If a note does not logically into a cluster post it off to the side as an "outlier".

5. Once the clusters are determined, discussion is allowed. Minor additional rearranging may occur at this time as participants clarify their understanding of what has been accomplished.

6. Once the clusters are clear and agreed upon, a label note or header is identified for each cluster. The header can be one of the cluster notes if it adequately summarizes the cluster information. If not, make up a header that does. The header must be specific and concise, a word or few words at the most, that captures the meaning of the cluster. Draw a boundary around the header using a color other than black to distinguish it from the cluster notes and place it at the top of the cluster.

7. Expand each header into a sentence that captures the essence of that particular cluster. If you are attempting to identify success criteria, mentally preface each sentence with the word *"when"* since the sentences should represent the evidences that are in place when whatever the group is working on has been successfully achieved.

It is often advantageous due to time considerations, and to allow for adequate quality thinking and interacting, to assign the task of expanding the headers into full sentences to a subgroup who will report back to the full group at a later time.

8. Finally, review your list. Are you satisfied? If not, what is missing? Or what modifications should be made?

Note:

A good application of the Affinity Diagram was described and illustrated in Chapter 4, Clarity: Developing Shared Expectations to identify and sort out work packages, and possibly related tasks, to construct a work breakdown structure in planning a project.

Fishbone Diagram

What It Is

The fishbone diagram, also known as the *Cause and Effect Diagram* or *Ishikawa Diagram*, named after its originator, is essentially structured mindmapping.

When to use

- When you need to identify and analyze potential causes of a problem.
- It is especially useful when working with a small group troubleshooting an issue.
- Complements intuition when analyzing problems.

How to use

1. Draw an arrow across the middle of the page.

2. Write a brief summary of the problem you want to analyze in a box to the right of the arrow.

3. Draw several diagonal lines from the main arrow to represent the major categories of potential causes of the problem. The categories will vary from problem to problem.

   A sample categorization is shown below.

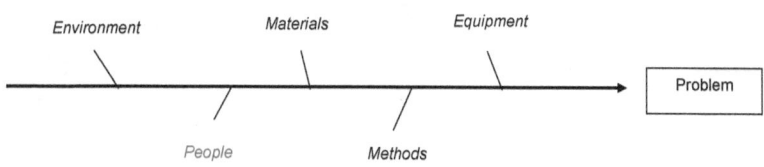

4. Focus on each of the major categories you have identified to fit the problem you are working on and list possible causes that fit with each category. List the possible causes on lines feeding into the major category.

For example:

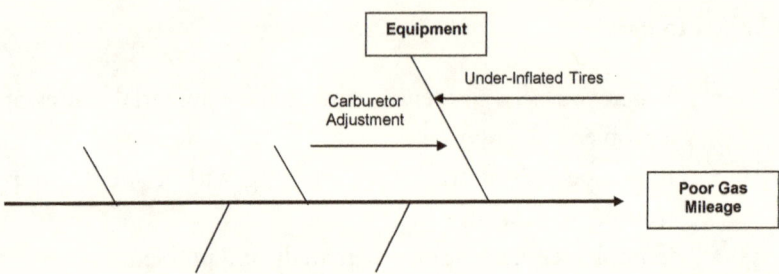

5. For each possible cause identified ask, "Why?", and list any appropriate responses as branches off of the major causes. Then ask "Why" again, and then again. This technique is commonly referred to as *The 5 Whys*. The idea again at this point is to identify potential causes of the problem. The next step will be to go back and try to identify the most likely cause or causes.

For Example:

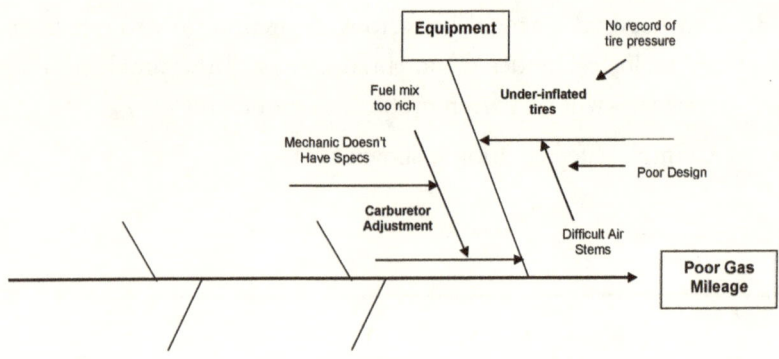

6. When you have completed the diagram, step back and analyze for root cause(s).

Whether you think you have identified the root cause(s) or not, you still may need to do further research to test and verify that you have indeed identified the root cause, or to gather more data to continue your research for causation.

<u>Tip:</u>

For more complex problems, the basic Fishbone Diagram can become too busy. For such applications use a separate piece of flipchart paper for each category of major cause identified, and do a mindmap of each. This variation of the tool accomplishes the same thing as a whole fishbone diagram, and is more fluid and easier to work with.

Functional Process Mapping

What It Is

A functional process map is a visual representation of a process that illustrates:

- What activities are completed by whom in what sequence.
- Hand-offs between departments or individuals.
- Internal and external operational boundaries or "swim lanes".
- Decision points.
- Clear starting and stopping points.

When to Use

- Diagnosing an existing process looking for areas to streamline or reengineer.
- Designing a new process.

How to Use

An example of a process map is shown below. The example shown is called a functional flow diagram in that it shows not only the process flow but also the various stakeholder groups or functions involved in the process. A flow diagram shows just the process flow, which is all you need if hand-offs between functions is not involved in the flow.

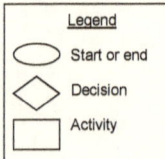

BUILDING BLOCK #4: TEAMS: SYNERGY AT WORK

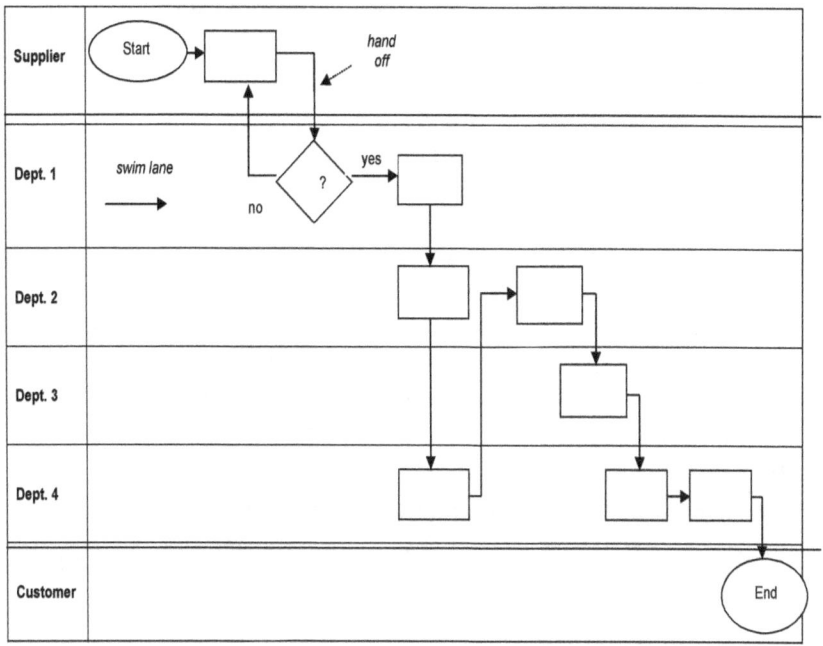

Note:

Functional Process Mapping is built upon the popular and useful Flow Diagram tool by including the various suppliers, such as, departments, groups, or individuals, involved in mapping out the process.

Narrowing the Number of Alternatives

Described below are two tools for narrowing the number of alternatives to a workable number to allow for quality thinking and interacting in making the final decision.

Multivoting

What It Is

Multivoting is a quick way to narrow down a list of ideas, options, or solutions to a workable number, for example, getting down to from three to five alternatives. Multivoting is exactly what it sounds like. Each member of the group can vote several times until the list is narrowed down to a workable number from which to make a decision.

How to Use

1. Assure that the group participants understand all the ideas that have been generated.

2. Eliminate duplications, combine similar ideas.

3. Number the remaining ideas.

4. Have participants vote on their top third of the ideas listed. Does not have to be 1/3, but 3 makes for a nice distribution.

   n/3: number of items listed divided by 3 = number of votes per participant

5. Tally the votes for each idea.

6. Circle the items receiving the highest number of votes.

BUILDING BLOCK #4: TEAMS: SYNERGY AT WORK

7. Count the number of circled items. If another round of voting is needed to narrow the list down to three to five items, repeat Step 4, using the n/3 formula.

8. Continue multivoting until you have the list down to three to five items. Never multivote down to a final decision. Instead use one of the Decision-Making tools described in this section, Pros and Cons or Decision Matrix, section to generate the necessary quality thinking and interacting to arrive at a decision that you have confidence in.

Nominal Group Technique

What It Is

The word "nominal" is used to describe this technique because when applying the group engages in only a minimal or nominal amount of interaction, giving group members equal voice.

When to use

To narrow down or decide upon the best idea(s), option(s), or solution(s) from a relatively short list, say no more than 10 choices, to a few that you can have quality thinking and interacting about to make an intelligent decision.

How to use

1. List and number or letter the ideas.

2. Assure that everyone understands each of the choices.

3. Tell the participants to individually write down his or her ranking of all the items on the list, with the highest priority assigned a value of 5, and the lowest a value of 1.

    For example:

Ideas	Rank
a.	4
b.	5 (highest rank)
c.	1 (lowest rank)
d.	3
e.	2

4. Have participants hand in their ranked list.

5. Tally results and record on a flipchart or board.

   For example:

Ideas	Votes	Totals	
a.	4,4,5,3,2	18	
b.	5,3,1,5,5,	19	← #1
c.	1,2,3,4,4	14	
d.	2,5,4,2,3	16	
e.	3,1,2,1,1	8	

6. Discuss results. Determine if further research is needed or if certain options need to be more thoroughly reviewed. For example, the closeness in voting for ideas a. and b. and possibly c. above would seem to indicate that further discussions were in order.

Action (or Project) Planning

What It Is

Action or project planning is a process for logically defining, communicating, and implementing a course of action to effectively achieve an objective or complete a project.

When to Use

When faced with a challenge, opportunity, or project that requires quality thinking and interacting to craft a logical and comprehensive course of action.

The Steps

1. **Project Specifications:** Defining Success

2. **Implementation Considerations:** What Lies Ahead?

3. **Work Breakdown Structure:** Identifying the Work Packages and Related Tasks

4. **Work Plan:** Sequencing and Detailing the Work to Be Done

Note:

Action (or Project) Planning is thoroughly discussed and illustrated in Chapter 4, Clarity: Defining Shared Expectations.

Some Final Thoughts on Tools

If desired, you can do a Google search and find out more about most of the tools discussed in this section as well as find additional tools you may be interested in. But, as mentioned earlier, my experience is that the tools discussed here are more than enough to do the job for most teams.

Use the appropriate tools to fit your application. If you are not accustomed to using process tools, do not fear. Just go ahead and dive in. Explain to the team what you are trying to do. They will want to help apply the tools and will not be looking for perfection. And the team members will, like you, delight in the benefits derived by using the tools, as well as the fun that can be gained in doing so.

Team Assessment

Appendix B, *Team Assessment* contains a questionnaire and related scoring designed to assess the effectiveness of a team. The questionnaire is built around the four building blocks–Results; Accountability; Collaboration; and Trust–that constitute the *Characteristics of a High-Performing Team* model shown in Figure 6.2, shown on pages 169-171.

CONCLUSION

To repeat what was said at the outset, there are two imperatives for growing an organization and sustaining success. These two imperatives apply to all business sectors. They also apply to the organization as a whole as well as specific organizational units.

The first imperative is a *sound strategy*. A strategy that clearly articulates both the organization's *Identity*, "Who we are"; and, "What we stand for"; and *Direction*, "Where we are going"; "What it looks like when we get there"; and, "How we are going to get there."

My book *Making and Fulfilling Your Dreams as a Leader: A Practical Guide for Formulating and Executing* Strategy[1] addresses the first imperative. Its purpose is to enable you as a leader, regardless of organizational level or business sector, to formulate and execute a sound strategy. The book equips you with a strategic framework to use on an ongoing basis to establish and live your organizational identity and direction in the face of current and emerging realities.

The second imperative is a work culture that fosters *genuine commitment*. That is what this book, *Building Commitment*, is all about. It is intended to serve as an ongoing guide to help you develop and sustain a committed workforce. A workforce where people "want to perform" rather than feeling that they "have to perform". Commitment rather than compliance. A committed workforce in which people want to work together to struggle to achieve shared aspirations.

This book provides you with the clarity, confidence, and competence to build and sustain such a workforce, now and in the future. Each of the book's four building blocks, Selection; Clarity; Performance Coaching; and, Teams, equips you with the requisite concepts, structures, processes, and tools to create and sustain a culture of commitment.

Hopefully, you have already applied many of these mechanisms in the course of reading the book, and have realized the results. And hopefully, you will continue to do so.

The book is intended to serve you well as a resource over time. A place to go to refresh yourself regarding using these important mechanisms as you encounter workforce opportunities and challenges.

The best of luck to you.

APPENDICES

APPENDIX A

THE ALEX REED CASE

Purpose

This case study is a practice vehicle for you to become familiar with the performance analysis logic described in Chapter 5, *Performance Coaching: Guiding Success*.

What to Do

1. Read the case study below.

2. Use the Performance Analysis model described in Chapter 5 to determine the cause and proper resolution of the performance discrepancy. Following the model, write down your analysis on paper as you work through the case..

3. Based on your analysis, what do you think the primary cause or causes of Alex's performance discrepancy is?

4. Based on your identification of causation, what would you do?

5. Compare your analysis with the analysis following the case. No fair peeking.

Alex Reed
Section Supervisor*

Alex Reed has been a supervisor at Pacific Enterprises for about two years. He came to the Electronics Division as a section supervisor after supervising for one year in the Plastics Division.

He seems to be a person who succeeds in whatever he tries. In school, he was always in the top 10% of his class, even though he worked and was active in athletics. He set several track records, and was an excellent boxer. He came to Pacific Enterprises after graduating from college.

Some people were hesitant about putting a man with no electronics experience in charge of a section, but Reed has done well. He has studied hard during the last two years, and developed a good working knowledge of the technical work of the two sections he has supervised.

Five months ago, Barney Simpson, Reed's immediate supervisor, completed a performance appraisal on him and conducted a very thorough counseling session. Simpson summarized Reed's performance during the previous year by citing some of his accomplishments and also by discussing some areas where there was room for improvement. Somewhat different from his previous performance review sessions, this discussion centered around the importance of accomplishing the performance standards that are established for the plant as a whole and for each supervisor. These standards are quantitative measures (ratios, percentages, etc.) which are intended to assess effectiveness in terms of production efficiency, cost control, employee turnover, and so on. Computer generated reports provide each supervisor with direct feedback on a weekly basis.

Reed has always met his individual performance standards, so they were raised slightly in an effort to compensate for the plant's overall performance, which has been lagging in several areas. The Plant Manager has asked everyone to make an extra effort to meet and exceed their individual performance standards.

In many respects Reed is one of the company's most outstanding employees. When he came to the division, he launched on his own initiative a vigorous cost reduction program. His section now presents a cost picture that makes the boss very happy.

Although a relatively new supervisor, Reed has a considerable amount of innate ability. He has very good relations with the people on his shift, even the old-timers who spoke derisively of "the kid" when he first came to work now like and respect him. He has convinced the people in his section that he has their best interests at heart and will go to bat for them. Turnover and absenteeism are lower in his section than in any other.

But the company pays a price for his talent. He is fiercely and single-mindedly determined to make his section the best one in the division. Unlike the other more experienced supervisors, Reed wants to be "number one" at any cost and he could not care less about the rest of the organization.

For example, on one occasion one of his machines broke down at a time when everyone was under pressure to get production out. He went to another section and found one of the maintenance men working on a broken machine there. He ordered the man to fix his machine. The man went to Reed's machine because, he later claimed, Reed said that the Supervisor of Maintenance had authorized it. Reed denied that he said this; nevertheless, his machine was fixed first.

APPENDIX A: THE ALEX REED CASE

When Reed needs the services of any of the organizational functions (engineering, accounting, human resources, etc.) his demands are often unreasonable, but he raises such a storm that, as one industrial engineer put it: "It's a whole lot easier to do what he asks and get him off your back."

Since the problem first started about five months ago, Reed has been involved in ten separate incidents with other supervisors or staff personnel. Reed's behavior is particularly irritating because it always seems to occur when everyone is under pressure to get production out. And when there are serious production problems, Reed is the only supervisor who is able to meet all of his performance standards, which naturally causes the other supervisors to be very resentful.

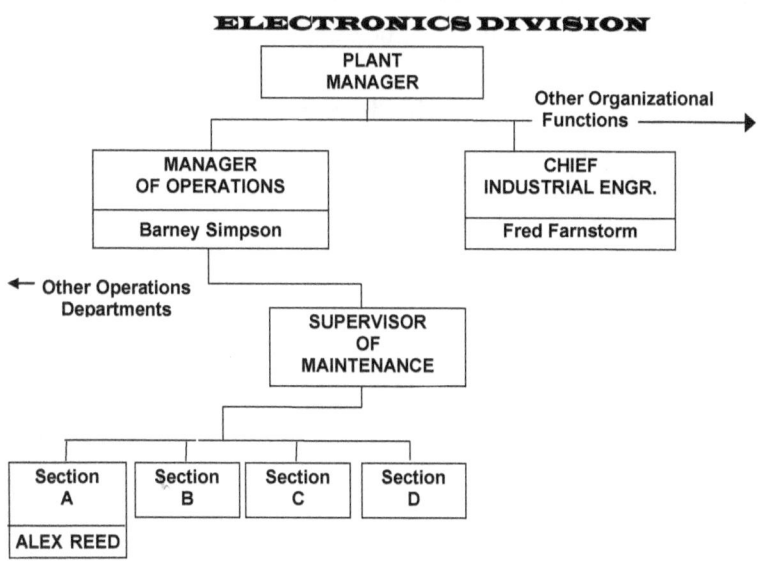

Most of the other supervisors dislike Reed. Some of them are beginning to respond to his lack of consideration and cooperation by treating him the same way, and the situation seems to be getting worse.

Their dislike for him is returned in kind. He thinks that they are not real supervisors, but overpaid technicians--they bumble and stumble along in their jobs and are envious of his success. The only time Reed gets along fairly well with some of his peers is when they bowl together on the company team.

Fred Farnstorm, the supervising industrial engineer, thinks that Reed is a valuable employee, but he tends to be a bit overzealous at times. Farnstorm has suggested to Simpson that Reed should be encouraged to take a good course in human relations. Simpson respects Farnstorm's opinion a great deal and he is considering acting on Farnstorm's suggestion.

Simpson has spoken to Reed several times about the way he acts. Reed always responds in the same way:

> "I know it gets people stirred up, but you've got to in order to get anything done around here. Besides, my record shows it's the right way, doesn't it? I'm better than these guys in every measurable way--in production, costs, turnover."

And it's true; he is better.

APPENDIX A: THE ALEX REED CASE

Author's Analysis of the Alex Reed Case

1. **Framing**

   The performance discrepancy

   > *How can I eliminate, or at least substantially decrease the tension between Alex and the other supervisors and organizational staff members and not lose Alex's contributions and commitment in doing so?*

   Importance

   > *Alex is being successful in achieving good results for his section. But his behavior and actions in doing so is having adverse effects on the Maintenance Department as a whole. The challenge is how to channel Alex's capabilities and motivation toward the good of the department as a whole without diminishing the results of the section,*

   What would happen if you did nothing?

   > *Left unchecked the situation will undoubtedly get much worse as Alex in driving his section continues to roll over other department and organizational staff members.*

BUILDING COMMITMENT

2. Gathering Intelligence

	IS *(the problem?)*	IS NOT *(the problem that could be?)*	CONTRASTS *(what, if anything, is unique, odd, or different about the IS and IS NOT data?)*
WHAT?	• Alex running rough shod over others to get his way. • Dislike and resent of Alex by other supervisors. • Alex looking down on other supervisors. • Potential that left unchecked Alex's continued behavior will have an adverse effect on overall department results.	• Alex's Section's results.	• Alex's section only section meeting performance standards.
WHO?	Alex	Other supervisors.	Alex is newest supervisor in the department and the least experienced.
WHERE?	• At work. • Electronics Division.	• Bowling team. • Plastics Division.	Different environments.
WHEN?	• Starting 5 months ago. • Problem more acute when everyone is under pressure to get production out.	• Before 5 months ago. • Less of a problem when not a big push on production.	• Stress placed on accomplishing quantitative performance standards for the plant as a whole and each supervisor. • Performance standards raised for Alex. • Alex thrives on meeting challenges.

EXTENT?	• 10 incidents with other supervisors and staff in last 5 months. • Situation getting worse. • Starting to be a backlash from other supervisors.		

3. Coming to Conclusions

Could Alex improve his work relationships with the other supervisors and organizational staff members if he really wanted to? That is the key question in determining whether the primary cause is a knowledge/skill deficiency, or beyond that an ability deficiency.

The answer to the question is "yes." Alex gets along fine on the bowling team. And, ostensibly there were no such relationships problems when he worked as a supervisor in the Plastics Division. So, we need to look at the environmental/motivational zone for the most likely cause of the performance discrepancy.

The key distinction is that the environments are different. The tangible performance standards have ignited Alex's intense achievement motivation and his desire to succeed at whatever he does. He will do anything to achieve the performance standards, as he is demonstrating.

So, the answer is not, as Fred Farnstorm recommended, training. Rather, the resolution is systemic. That is, understanding and appreciating Alex and his talents and makeup, and the current work environment he is operating in. And then thinking through what kinds of changes might be appropriate to resolve the performance discrepancy.

There are several strategies that would seem to be appropriate in attempting to resolve this performance discrepancy.

The first is that Barney needs to make sure that Alex understands and accepts the performance expectations when it comes to establishing and maintaining effective working relationships. Not only with his people, but the world around him. Alex may not agree with these performance expectations, at least initially, but he needs to accept them, and follow them.

In this regard, Barney could benefit from the discussions in Chapter 2, Clarity: Developing Shared Expectations, on the importance of clarifying leadership and management expectations as well as technical work expectations.

The second strategy that makes a lot of sense is to restructure the performance standards so they focus on the Maintenance Division as a whole rather than the individual sections. Doing so, would both be an imperative for both building a high-performing team by providing a common focus, as well as channeling Alex's talents and passions so that he might positively contribute to the common good.

In this regard, Barney could benefit from spending some quality time with Chapter 6, Teams: Synergy at Work and the guidelines provided for developing high-performing teams.

In addition to structuring a common-results focus for the Maintenance Division, Barney should look for opportunities to have the maintenance supervisors as well as other maintenance employees work together on collective work products that will benefit the division. There may be opportunities in so doing for Alex to take a project lead and for Barney to provide effective performance coaching.

4. **Implementing**

   It would make sense for Barney to first do some quality thinking and perhaps interacting regarding moving toward division performance standards in beginning to build an effective team. The performance coaching conversations with Alex will be more productive if this transformation has been thought through and Barney is willing and able to implement it. Once Barney is convinced of the wisdom of making this transformation he can work with Alex and the other supervisors in developing and implementing the division's performance standards.

   Next, he will want to look for opportunities for collective work products, which will be an ongoing strategy for not only improving the division's performance, but for also building an effective leadership team.

5. **Learning from Experience**

   This case illustrates the importance of taking a systemic approach in attempting to resolve not only performance discrepancies, but any problem that pops up.

   All too often when dealing with people problems managers will gravitate to quick and simple solutions rather than do the needed quality thinking to identify and treat the root cause or causes of the problem. Examples include jumping to training or disciplinary solutions. Managers like the feeling they get from such action-oriented activities because they think they are doing something to solve the problem. This is not to say that training and disciplinary action are not called for in some instances, but only when such actions truly address the cause of the problem.

BUILDING COMMITMENT

The astute manager attempts to peel back the skin of the onion in search of the root cause or causes of a problem. Frequently the person with the problem will have competing commitments. That is, they may want to resolve the problem, but other commitments, be they innate or learned, may get in the way. And often the person with the problem is unaware that such competing commitments even exist. A manager who can help a person discover such competing conflicts and constructively deal with them is truly doing a yeoman's job in providing professional performance coaching.

In our case study, Alex's high level of achievement motivation and his competitive nature has led to the work relationship issues. He will do anything to meet those tangible technical performance standards. The potential solutions as recommended above can effectively deal with such competing commitments by making some important structural changes in the performance expectations. And in rechanneling Alex's talents and passion toward achieving these expectations he will be able to provide higher value contributions.

APPENDIX B
TEAM ASSESSMENT

The *Team Assessment* is designed to give you a general assessment of just how you and your team think it stacks up relative to each of the four Building Blocks–Results; Accountability; Collaboration; and Trust–that constitute the *Characteristics of a High-Performing Team* model discussed in Chapter 6, *Teams: Synergy at Work,* pages 169-171. The assessment provides you with an idea of just how you and your team perceive its strengths and areas needing improvement.

The team assessment components listed below are shown on the following pages.

Team Assessment Questionnaire	To be completed by the team leader and each team member.
Team Assessment Worksheet	Worksheet to: • List individual scores for each Statement. • Compute team score for each Statement. • Compute team score for each Building Block

- Recommend the team leader along with a team member work together using the Team Assessment Worksheet to compute the team results.

- Plan to compute the results soon after the team members have completed and turned in their individual assessments. Before handing in their assessments, have each member make note of their individual scores for the 16 Statements. In doing so, they can compare their individual scores to the team scores once the results are tallied, distributed, and discussed.

TEAM ASSESSMENT QUESTIONNAIRE

What to Do

Use the scale below to rate your assessment of your team for each statement. Evaluate the statements honestly. Do not overthink your answers.

Strongly Agree		Somewhat Agree			Strongly Disagree
5	4	3	2	1	

_____ 1. As opportunities present themselves, team members work on projects together.

_____ 2. Team members are willing to make personal or departmental sacrifices for the good of the team.

_____ 3. The reason the team exists is clear.

_____ 4. Team members understand the roles they are expected to play on the team.

_____ 5. Team members fully participate in resolving important issues.

_____ 6. Team members are open and honest with one another.

_____ 7. The desired future state the team is striving to achieve is clear.

_____ 8. Team members are very concerned about not letting the team down.

_____ 9. The team's goals are clear.

_____ 10. Team members understand and appreciate their individual uniqueness and effectively make use of such differences.

____ 11. The team periodically assesses how effectively its members work together.

____ 12. Team meetings are productive.

____ 13. The team uses common processes to facilitate quality thinking and interacting in solving problems, making decisions, and planning actions.

____ 14. Progress in achieving the teams' desired results are assessed on a regular basis.

____ 15. Expected team behaviors in conducting team business are understood.

____ 16. Team members can count on one another to come through

APPENDIX B: TEAM ASSESSMENT

TEAM ASSESSMENT WORKSHEET
BUILDING BLOCK: RESULTS

Team Scores for Each Statement

Statements	Individual Team Member Scores	Total of Individual Scores	÷	# Team Members	=	Ave. Team Score for Statement
3.						
7.						
9.						
14.						

Team Score for the RESULTS Building Block

Total Team Score for the Statements (Add up Ave. Team Scores from the last column above)	÷	# Team Members	=	Team Score for Building Block

BUILDING COMMITMENT

TEAM ASSESSMENT WORKSHEET
BUILDING BLOCK: ACCOUNTABILITY

Team Scores for Each Statement

Statements	Individual Team Member Scores	Total of Individual Scores	÷	# Team Members	=	Ave. Team Score for Statement
4.						
8.						
11.						
15.						

Team Score for the ACCOUNTABILITY Building Block

Total Team Score for the 4 Statements (Add up Ave. Team Scores from the last column above)	÷	# Team Members	=	Team Score for Building Block

APPENDIX B: TEAM ASSESSMENT

TEAM ASSESSMENT WORKSHEET
BUILDING BLOCK: COLLABORATION

Team Scores for Each Statement

Statements	Individual Team Member Scores	Total of Individual Scores	÷	# Team Members	=	Ave. Team Score for Statement
1.						
5.						
12.						
13.						

Team Score for the COLLABORATION Building Block

Total Team Score for the 4 Statements (Add up the Team Scores from the last column above)	÷	# of Team Members	=	Team Score for Building Block

245

BUILDING COMMITMENT

TEAM ASSESSMENT WORKSHEET
BUILDING BLOCK: TRUST

Team Scores for Each Statement

Statements	Individual Team Member Scores	Total of Individual Scores	÷	# Team Members	=	Ave. Team Score for Statement
2.						
6.						
10.						
16.						

Team Score for the TRUST Building Block

Total Team Score for the 4 Statements (Add up the Team Scores from the last column above)	÷	# of Team Members	=	Team Score for Building Block

ANALYSIS

What to Do

Use the Team Assessment Worksheets to conduct the analysis.

Recommend the team leader individually analyze the data. Then, facilitate a review, analysis, and discussion with the team. Make it timely. Do not let too much time pass between the team members completing the assessments and getting back to them.

Score Interpretation

Score

5 – 9	This Statement or Building Block definitely needs attention.
10 – 15	This Statement or Building Block may warrant some attention.
16 -20	This Statement or Building Block is going well.

Steps

- Identify any notable distinctions between the team leader's scores and the team scores. If such distinctions exist, what might they indicate?

- Identify any notable variances amongst the team scores for each of the 16 Statements. If such variances exist, what might they signify?

- When considering possible areas for improvement and related strategies and actions for doing so for a specific Building Block, review:

- The Average Team Score for each of the Statements for that Building Block.
- Applicable Structures; Helpful Mechanisms; and, Effective Interactions listed in Chapter 6, *Teams: Synergy at Work* for high-performing teams, pages 170-172.

- Identify areas for improvement.

- Craft and implement appropriate improvement plans.

- Monitor and, as appropriate, modify results.

It is a good practice to retake the Team Assessment periodically. Perhaps annually. Realize that changes in team membership will have a bearing on future results.

ENDNOTES

Introduction
1. Carl Welte, *Making and Fulfilling Your Dreams as a Leader: A Practical Guide for Formulating and Executing Strategy,* Second Edition, The Ewings Publishing, 2022.

Chapter One
1. Jeffrey Pfeffer, *The Human Equation: Building Profits by Building People First,* Harvard Business School Press, 1998.
2. Charles A. O'Reilly III and Jeffrey Pfeffer, *Hidden Value: How Great Companies Achieve Extraordinary Results with Ordinary People,* Harvard Business School Press, 2000.
3. Patrick Lencioni. *The Advantage: Why Organizational Health Trumps Everything Else in Business,* Jossey-Bass, 2012.
4. The Gallup Organization, *2022 State of the American Workplace.* Report available as a download from www.Gallup.com.
5. Pfeffer, op. cit.
6. In 2012 Dale Carnegie & Associates, Inc. contracted with MSW Research to conduct a nationwide study involving focusing on employee engagement and involving 1,500 employees. The results of the study can be found in two white papers available as downloads from www.dalecarnegie.com. The titles of the white papers are: *"Engaging Employees: What Drives Employee Engagement and Why It Matters",* and, *"Enhancing Employee Engagement: The Role of the Immediate Supervisor".*

7. James M. Kouzes and Barry Z. Posner, *The Leadership Challenge: How to Make Extraordinary Things Happen in Organizations,* Sixth Edition, Jossey-Bass, 2017.

Chapter Two
1. Abraham H. Maslow, *A Theory of Human Motivation.* A 2013 reprint of the 1943 article in which Maslow first presented his hierarchy of needs.
2. Wayne W. Dyer, *I Can See Clearly Now,* Hay House, 2014.
3. Peter F. Drucker, *Management Challenges for the 21st Century,* Harper Business, 1999.
4. Frederick Herzberg, Bernard Mausner, and Barbara Bloch Snyderman, *The Motivation to Work,* Transaction Publishers, Reprint Edition, 1993. Originally published: Wiley, 1959.
5. Frederick Herzberg, *Work and the Nature of Man,* Thomas Y. Crowell Co., 1966.
6. Frederic Herzberg, "One More Time: How Do You Motivate Employees?", *Harvard Business Review* (January-February 1968).
7. Raymond E. Miles and W.E. Creed, "Organizational Forms and Managerial Philosophies: A Descriptive and Analytical Review, *Research in Organizational Behavior, Volume 17, pages 333-372* (1995).
Raymond E. Miles and Charles C. Snow, *Fit, Failure and the Hall of Fame: How Companies Succeed or Fail,* The Free Press, 1994.
Raymond E. Miles, *Theories of Management,* McGraw-Hill, 1975.
8. Douglas McGregor, *The Human Side of Enterprise,* McGraw-Hill, 1960.

Chapter Three
1. Lyle and Signa Spencer's book, *Competence at Work: Models for Superior Performance,* John Wiley & Sons, Inc., 1993 was valuable in helping me shape my thinking regarding the types of Position Success Factors.

2. Peter Thiel with Blake Masters, *Zero to One: Notes on Startups, or How to Build the Future*, Crown Business, 2014.
3. Claudio Fernandez-Araoz, "21st Century Talent Spotting", *Harvard Business Review* (June 2014).
4. Robert F. Mager, *Goal Analysis*, Fearon Publishers/Lear, 1972.
5. Mark Murphy, "The Hidden Flaw in Behavioral Interview Questions", *Forbes* magazine blog, January 2015.

Chapter Four

1. Carl Welte, op. cit.
2. Thanks to my long-time valued mentor and colleague Ralph Bettman for exposing me to the position planning logic some years ago. Ralph and I successfully used this solid planning logic with a variety of client professionals. Since then time I have made some minor improvements to the logic and have continued to use this planning logic with a variety of clients at all organizational levels in all business sectors to help them gain clarity regarding their roles and responsibilities.
3. James M. Kouzes and Barry Z. Posner, op.cit.
4. Adapted from: Robert F. Mager, op.cit.
5. Brian Tracy, *Goals!: How to Get Everything You Want–Faster than You Ever Thought Possible*, Berrett-Koehler, 2003.

Chapter Five

1. Bruce Tulgan, *It's Okay to Be the Boss: The Step-by-Step Guide to Becoming the Manager Your Employees Need*, Collins Business, 2007.
2. *Managing by Walking Around* (MBWA) has been a recommended management practice for some time. Jim Kouzes and Barry Posner, known for their research and writing on leadership, renamed the practice to *Caring by Walking Around* (CBWA). The word "caring" greatly enhances the meaning of what this practice should be all about. It is true that you can get a lot of valuable input from direct observations, but the word caring connotes that you are also out there genuinely looking for

opportunities to provide just in time help to your people, in addition to gathering intelligence regarding what is going on.
3. I have put my own spin on the GROW Model developed by: Max Landsberg, *The Tao of Coaching: Boost Your Effectiveness by Inspiring Those Around You*, Knowledge Exchange, 1997.
4. Adapted from: William Oncken, Jr. and Donald L. Wass, *Management Time: Who's Got the Monkey*, Harvard Business Review, (November-December 1999.)
5. Michael Csikszentmihalyi, *finding Flow: The Psychology of Engagement with Everyday Life*, Basic Books, 1997.
6. Frederick Herzberg, *Work and the Nature of Man*, op.cit.
7. The genesis of the *Performance Analysis* model sprung from a book by Bob Mager, a foremost instructional technologist. The book: Robert F. Mager and Peter Pipe, *Analyzing Performance Problems or "You Really Oughta Wanna"*, Fearon Pitman Publishers, Inc., 1970. As good as Mager's model is, it is limited for managers in that its primary focus is to determine whether or not a skill efficiency to assess whether training is appropriate. In my experience, a supervising manager needs a more robust model to cope with the variety of performance discrepancies he is likely to encounter.
8. Adapted from: Geary Rummler and Alan Bache, *Improving Performance: How to Manage the White Space on the Organization Chart*, Jossey-Bass, Inc. 1990.
9. J. Edward Russo and Paul J.H. Schoemaker, *Winning Decisions: Getting It Right the First Time,* Currency Doubleday, 2002.

Chapter Six

1. Adapted from: Gil Amelio and William Simon, *Profit from Experience: The National Semiconductor Story of Transformation Management*, Reinhold, 1996.
2. The stages of team development listed here is a long-standing model developed by Bruce Tuckman in 1965. The fifth stage, Adjournment, was added in 1075.
Bruce Tuckman, "Developmental Sequence in Small Groups", *Psychological Bulletin 63, pp. 384-399 (1965).*

3. Carl Welte, op.cit.
4. J.Allen McCarthy, *Genius, Innovation & Luck: The "Rocket Science of Building High-Performance Corporations,* 4th Edition Publishing, 2011.
5. Ray Dalio, *Principles*, Simon & Schuster, 2017.
6. Sam Kaner with Lenny Lind, Catherine Toldi, Sarah Fisk, and Duane Berger, *Facilitor's Guide to Participatory Decision-Making*, New Society Publishers, 1996.
7. Robert F. Mager, *Goal Analysis*, op. cit.
8. Charles H. Kepner and Benjamin B Tregoe, *The Rational Manager: A Systematic Approach to Problem Solving and Decision Making*, 1976.
9. J. Edward Russo and Paul J.H. Schoemaker, op. cit.
10. Charles H. Kepner and Benjamin B. Tregoe, op. cit.

Conclusion
1. Carl Welte, op. cit.

ABOUT THE AUTHOR

Carl Welte founded Welte Associates in 1993. Welte Associates enables organizational leaders and teams to achieve desired business results by helping them build the organizational capabilities to do so.

His more than fifty years of organizational, management, and consulting experience has equipped him with the requisite wisdom and coaching skills to enable leaders and teams to effectively address their organization's opportunities and challenges.

He has held senior-level positions in both large and small organizations. Carl has also held leadership positions in a variety of professional, industrial, and educational associations.

Carl was a visiting faculty member for 12 years at the University of Idaho, teaching in its executive development program. He has also taught leadership and management programs in the University of California's extension learning system for more than 10 years.

He is the author of *Making and Fulfilling Your Dreams as a Leader: A Practical Guide for Formulating and Executing Strategy*, Second Edition, The Ewings Publishing, 2022; *Building Commitment: A Leader's Guide to Unleashing the Human Potential at Work*, Second Edition, The Ewings Publishing, 2022; and, *Communicating about Differences: Understanding, Appreciating, and Talking about Divergent Points of View*, Second Edition, The Ewings Publishing, 2022.

He has an MBA from the University of California, Berkeley, and a BS degree in business administration from the University of California.

Carl lives in Novato, CA with his wife Dee. They have three children, six Grandchildren, and one great grandchild.

He can be reached at:

> Welte Associates
> 14 Plata Court
> Novato, CA 94947
> Phone: (415) 328-1349
> Email: carl@welte.com
> Website: welte.com

www.ingramcontent.com/pod-product-compliance
Lightning Source LLC
LaVergne TN
LVHW041755060526
838201LV00046B/1013